unexpected crochet for the home

Vice President and Chief Operations Officer: Tom Siebenmorgen
Vice President, Sales and Marketing: Pam Stebbins
Vice President, Operations: Jim Dittrich
Editor in Chief: Susan White Sullivan
Director of Designer Relations: Debra Nettles
Senior Art Director: Rhonda Shelby
Senior Prepress Director: Mark Hawkins

Produced for Leisure Arts, Inc. by Penn Publishing Ltd.
www.penn.co.il
Editor: Shoshana Brickman
Technical editing: Rita Greenfeder
Design and layout: Ariane Rybski
Photography by: Michal Lenart
Styling: Amit Farber
Special thanks to Neve Tsedek Hotel, Tel Aviv

PRINTED IN CHINA

ISBN-13: 978-1-57486-326-0
ISBN-10: 1-57486-326-6
Library of Congress Control Number: 2009940832

Cover photography by Michal Lenart

unexpected crochet for the home

by

LENA MAIKON

A LEISURE ARTS PUBLICATION

contents

introduction

Fields of flowers and leaf-covered forest floors, rows of planted vegetables and colorful dried gourds—these are just some of the elements that inspire the projects in **Unexpected Crochet for the Home**. Natural materials and simple crochet stitches are complemented with non-traditional crochet techniques to create contemporary home accessories that are a pleasure to make, lovely to touch, and just right for decorating a modern home.

The projects integrate diverse materials such as bamboo, recycled cotton, and jute rope to plastic fabric, steel rods, and wire. As for techniques, several projects involve crocheting over rope, allowing for the construction of flexible yet sturdy vessels and containers. Once you are familiar with this technique, you'll find an entire world of new crochet possibilities open to you!

There are accessories for outfitting every room in your house—cushion covers, a rug, and a couch covering for your living room or family room; lampshades and wall hangings for your study or hallway. A distinct runner, apron, and oven mitt are just right for the kitchen or dining room; slippers and a stuffed toy are ideal for the bedroom. There are also vases, containers, and more, objects to suit any room in your house.

If you are looking for a small project, you might choose to make a crocheted chamomile or chrysanthemum, or a small vase for holding real flowers. If you're looking for a project that requires a bit more time, choose a foot-warming rug or large wall hanging.

All of the projects are connected to nature, evoking the natural world much like an impressionist painting; in other words, they aren't meant to copy nature exactly, but are reminiscent of nature in their colors, textures, and shapes. Many are connected to the seasons as well. Looking for something wintry? A pair of warm slippers may be just right. When spring is in the air, you may feel like making a soft sheep or a small flowery field wall hanging. A large lampshade is a perfect project for the long days of summer; bright cushion covers embody the vibrant colors of autumn.

about the author

Lena Maikon learned to knit and crochet from her grandmother at the age of five in her hometown of Novosibrisk, Russia. She picked up the hobby again many years later, as a form of creative therapy. This quickly turned into a passion and profession. Lena often uses unconventional materials in her designs, and dreams of creating a knitted and crocheted world. She crafts socks, shoes, dresses, handbags, flowers, vases, and light fixtures using not-so-traditional techniques. Lena has published four creative knitting and crocheting books, and has her own handmade clothing and accessory label, Leninka. Lena is the mother of two young sons.

essentials

standard yarn weight system

Yarn Weight Symbol & Names	LACE 0	SUPER FINE 1	FINE 2	LIGHT 3	MEDIUM 4	BULKY 5	SUPER BULKY 6
Type of Yarns in Category	Fingering, size 10 crochet thread	Sock, Fingering, Baby	DK, Light Worsted	DK, Light Worsted	Worsted, Afghan, Aran	Chunky, Craft, Rug	Bulky, Roving

*GUIDELINES ONLY: The chart above reflects the most commonly used gauges and needle sizes for specific yarn categories.

** Lace weight yarns are usually knitted on larger needles to create lacy openwork patterns. Accordingly, a gauge range is difficult to determine. Always follow the gauge stated in your pattern.

CROCHET TERMINOLOGY

United States	International
slip stitch (slip st)	single crochet (sc)
single crochet (sc)	double crochet (dc)
half double crochet (hdc)	half treble crochet (htc)
double crochet (dc)	treble crochet (tr)
treble crochet (tr)	double treble crochet (dtr)
treble double crochet (dtr)	triple treble crochet (ttr)
triple treble crochet (tr tr)	quadruple treble crochet (qtr)
skip	miss

SKILL LEVELS

■□□□ Beginner	Projects for first-time crocheters using basic stitches. Minimal shaping.
■■□□ Easy	Projects using yarn with basic stitches, repetitive stitch patterns, simple color changes, and simple shaping and finishing.
■■■□ Intermediate	Projects using a variety of techniques, such as basic lace patterns or color patterns, mid-level shaping and finishing.
■■■■ Experienced	Projects with intricate stitch patterns, techniques and dimension, suxh as non-repeating patterns, multi-color techniques, fine threads, small hooks, detailed shapping and refined finishing.

CROCHET HOOKS

U.S.	B-0	C-2	D-3	E-4	F-5	G-6	H-7	I-9	J-10	K-10½	N	P	Q
METRIC - MM	2.25	2.75	3.25	3.5	3.75	4	5	5.5	6	6.5	9	10	15

Yarn selection

To make an exact replica of the photographed items, use the yarns listed in the Materials and Tools section of the projects. All of the yarns in these projects are readily available in the United States and Canada. Feel free to substitute them with yarns of your preference. Remember that with a different yarn, you'll need to adjust the crochet gauge to the measurements specified in the project instructions. Consider in advance whether you'll need to adjust the quantity of yarn for your project, especially if you're ordering the yarn online.

Gauge

Crochet a gauge swatch before beginning any project. If you want to obtain the exact results described, you must reach the gauge listed for that project. Try using different crochet hook sizes for the gauge, experimenting and measuring until your swatch contains the required number of stitches and rows. If you want fewer stitches per inch/cm, use larger hooks; if you want more, use smaller hooks.

Crochet a gauge swatch before beginning any project. If you want to obtain the exact results described, you must reach the gauge listed for that project. Try using different crochet hook sizes for the gauge, experimenting and measuring until your swatch contains the number of stitches and rows indicated. If you want fewer stitches per inch/cm, use larger hooks; if you want more, use smaller hooks.

Don't be surprised that I often use hooks smaller than those recommended for a specific yarn. Though it may be more difficult to crochet with a smaller hook, I choose to do so deliberately to create a "fabric" that is durable and holds its shape.

Blocking

This is done to shape the crocheted piece. Place a damp cloth on wrong side of crocheted piece, and a hot iron on top. Wait a few seconds, until damp cloth is dry.

special materials and tools

Multi-ply soft jute rope

This is used in several projects to create a sturdy structure. Made from plant fiber, jute rope holds it shape well, and can be washed. However, it can also be broken, so take care how it is handled. Look for jute rope that has a diameter of $\frac{5}{32}$"/4mm to $\frac{3}{16}$"/5mm. Using rope that is thinner (or thicker) will change the final measurement of the project.

Leather and leather hole punch

Leather is used for the soles in the Forest Floor Slippers. The hole punch is used to punch holes in leather for these slippers, and for the plastic cover in the Sunny Sunflower Apron.

Clear plastic fabric

This is used to protect the Sunny Sunflower Apron. It can be found in many craft stores and fabric supply shops.

Wire and wire cutters

The wire is used to make flexible stems in several projects.

Lamp frame

This is used for the Large and Small Luminous Pod lampshades. If you can't find a readymade lamp frame that fits your crocheted lampshade, order a custom-made lamp frame online to match your specifications.

Basic standing lamp electricity kit

This is used to provide light in the Large and Small Luminous Pod lampshades. They are readily available at stores and online.

Steel rods

This is used to make a sturdy frame for the Strips of Sprouts Wall Hanging. It must be made to measure, so have it cut to size after you have completed crocheting the project. Most lumber stores will be able to do this on site.

special stitches

Overlay chain stitch (overlay ch)

Insert hook into work, from front to back, in stitch indicated.

Yarn over.

Draw yarn through work and loop on hook.

Reverse single crochet stitch (reverse sc)

Working left to right, insert hook in next stitch to the right.

Yarn over, draw yarn through stitch.

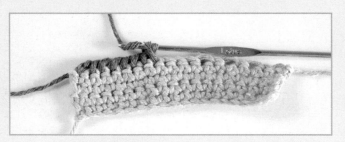

Yarn over, draw yarn through 2 loops on hook to complete stitch.

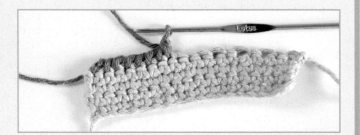

Picot (Bud)

Chain 3 (4).

Insert hook in third (fourth) chain from hook.

Yarn over and draw through stitch and loop on hook to complete stitch.

Skip next stitch, slip stitch in next stitch (or as indicated).

Loop stitch (Loop st)

Note: Stitch is created on backside while working.

Wrap yarn around index finger, insert hook in next stitch, and grab yarn under index finger.

Pull up a loop, leaving formed loop over index finger. Drop loop to backside and pick up end of yarn.

Draw through both loops on hook to complete stitch.

Puff stitch (Puff st)

Yarn over, insert hook in next stitch (or as indicated).

Yarn over, pull up a loop, yarn over.

(Insert hook in same stitch and yarn over, pull up a loop, yarn over) three times.

Draw through all loops on hook.

Chain 1 to complete stitch.

techniques

Adjustable ring

Wrap yarn twice around index finger to make a double loop a few inches from end of yarn, leaving a tail in front.

Insert hook into double loop, from front to back. Yarn over.

Draw working yarn through double loop, so there is one loop on hook.

Chain 1.

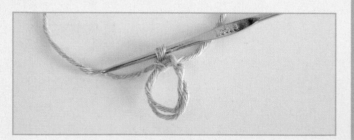

Work 6 single crochet (or as indicated) into double loop, crocheting over double loop and tail.

Pull tail snugly to close ring.

Join with slip stitch in first single crochet to complete ring.

Attaching to frame

With right side of crocheted frame facing and yarn behind frame, insert hook in indicated unused loop of foundation chains at inner side of frame closest to you. Yarn over and pull up a loop.

Chain and work as indicated.

With loop on hook, insert hook in indicated unused loop of foundation chains at inner side of frame farthest from you. Yarn over. Draw through both loops on hook to complete overlay chain stitch.

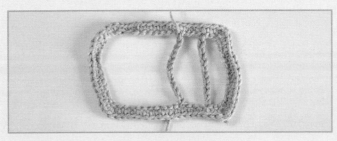

Fasten off.

Weaving ropes into foundation net

With right side of foundation net facing and yarn behind net, insert hook in indicated single crochet at edge of net, on side closest to you. Yarn over and pull up a loop. Work overlay chains as indicated in each next 'single crochet' row.

Chain as indicated to complete a rope.

Remove hook from loop. Leave untied large loop and cut yarn, leaving a 5"/12.5cm tail.

Weave rope in and out of each square along length (width) of foundation net.

Insert hook in large loop, tighten loop, and bringing yarn behind net, insert hook in indicated stitch. Yarn over. Draw through both loops on hook to complete first overlay chain stitch. Work overlay chains as indicated in each next 'single crochet' row.

Foundation row over rope

Fold yarn to create a loop, leaving a 2"/5cm tail. Place folded yarn on rope, 1"/2.5cm (or as indicated) left from free end of rope. Insert hook into loop and above rope.

Bringing yarn behind rope, yarn over, grabbing working yarn and tail together (or working yarn only).

Draw two strands of yarn (or working yarn only) through loop on hook to complete a chain over rope stitch.

Bringing hook under rope, holding rope and yarn tail together, yarn over and pull up a loop.

Bringing hook above rope, holding rope and yarn tail together, yarn over and draw through both loops on hook to complete a single crochet over rope stitch.

Work single crochet over rope stitches as indicated to complete a foundation row over rope.

Foundation round over rope

Make a foundation row over rope, working single crochet over rope stitches as indicated in pattern instructions.

Curve foundation row into a ring, carrying working rope and yarn above foundation row. Insert hook in first single crochet of foundation row.

Bringing yarn behind rope, yarn over and pull up a loop. Bringing hook above rope, yarn over and draw through both loops on hook to complete a single crochet over rope stitch and to connect ring.

Attaching rope to foundation chains

With free end of rope to your right, place rope above foundation chains. Insert hook in first chain of foundation chains. Yarn over and pull up a loop. With yarn behind rope, bringing hook above rope, yarn over and draw through loop on hook to complete a chain over rope stitch.

Insert hook in next chain of foundation chains.

Yarn over and pull up a loop. Bringing hook above rope, yarn over and draw through both loops on hook to complete single crochet over rope stitch.

Single crochet over rope (sc over rope)

With rope above last row (or round) and yarn behind rope, insert hook in next stitch.

Yarn over and pull up a loop.

Bringing hook above rope, yarn over and draw through both loops on hook to complete stitch.

Chain above rope, single crochet over rope (ch above rope, sc over rope)

With rope above last row (or round) and yarn behind rope, bringing hook above rope, chain 1 above rope (or as indicated). Skip next stitch. Insert hook in next stitch (or as indicated).

Make 1 single crochet over rope (or stitch indicated).

Long single crochet over rope (lsc over rope)

With rope above last row (or round) and yarn behind rope, insert hook in next stitch, 1 row (or round) below.

Yarn over and pull up a long loop.

Bringing hook above rope, yarn over and draw through both loops on hook to complete stitch.

Half double crochet over rope (hdc over rope)

With rope above last row (or round) and yarn behind rope, bringing hook above rope, yarn over. Insert hook in next stitch.

Yarn over and pull up a loop. Bringing hook above rope, yarn over and draw through all 3 loops on hook to complete stitch.

Double crochet over rope (dc over rope)

With rope above last row (or round) and yarn behind the rope, bringing hook above rope, yarn over. Insert hook in next stitch. Yarn over and pull up a loop. Bringing hook above rope, yarn over and draw through 2 loops on hook.

Bringing hook above rope, yarn over and draw through 2 loops on hook to complete stitch.

Attaching rope to leather piece

Position rope on leather piece, with free end to your right, and behind holes.

Insert hook in first hole. Yarn over and pull up a loop. Bringing yarn behind rope and hook above rope, yarn over and draw through loop on hook to complete a chain over rope stitch.

Insert hook in next hole.

Yarn over and pull up a loop.

Bringing yarn behind rope and hook above rope, yarn over and draw through both loops on hook to complete single crochet over rope stitch.

Crocheting petals in a round

Insert hook in next stitch at last round of flower center (or as indicated). Slip stitch.

Chain as indicated at first row of petal instructions.

Work second row of petal as indicated, making last slip stitch in same stitch as at beginning of first row of petal.

Making a flexible stem with rootlets

With wrong side of flower facing, make an overhand knot flush against flower center in longer rope end.

Insert 1"/2.5cm of wire in knot, from bottom of knot towards flower, and fold over thinner part of knot.

With flower to the right, holding rope, wire, and 3"/7.5cm free end of hemp yarn together with one hand, use other hand to wrap hemp yarn tightly, starting to right of knot, covering knot and folded wire, and continuing along rope and wire until end of wire.

With hemp yarn, tie an overhand knot over rope. Cut hemp yarn and rope, leaving a 5"/12.5cm tail on each.

Separate rope tail into sections, and join hemp yarn to one section.

Make an overhand knot in each section, flush against bottom of stem.

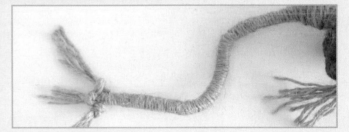

Trim ends, leaving a 1"/2.5cm tail on each, and fray.

19

terms and abbreviations

approx	approximately
beg	begin
ch above rope, sc over rope	chain above rope, single crochet over rope
ch(s)	chain stitch(es)
cm	centimeter(s)
cont	continue
dc	double crochet
dc over rope	double crochet over rope
g	grams
hdc	half double crochet
hdc over rope	half double crochet over rope
htr	half treble crochet
Loop st	Loop Stitch
lp(s)	loop(s)
lsc	long single crochet
lsc over rope long	single crochet over rope
m	meter(s)
mm	millimeter
overlay ch(s)	overlay chain stitch(es)
oz	ounce
prev	previous
Puff st	Puff Stitch
rem	remaining
rep	repeat
reverse sc	reverse single crochet stitch
rnd(s)	round(s)
RS	right side
sc over rope	single crochet over rope

sc	single crochet
sc2tog	single crochet two together
sk	skip
sl st	slip stitch
st(s)	stitch(es)
tog	together
tr	treble crochet
WS	wrong side
yd	yard
*(**, ***)	repeat instructions following the single (double, triple) asterisk as many times as written

comfy couch throw

This soft throw blanket brings the rich colors of autumn inside, while keeping you wrapped up and warm. Perfect for decorating a couch or chair, it will also keep you warm when you snuggle up with a good book. Impressive, yet quick and easy to make.

EXPERIENCE LEVEL

■■□□ Easy

FINISHED MEASUREMENTS

- 50"/127cm x 85"/216cm

MATERIALS AND TOOLS

- Yarn A **(4 MEDIUM)**: 1,539yd/1,404m of Medium weight yarn, cotton, in dark brown
- Yarn B **(4 MEDIUM)**: 342yd/312m of Medium weight yarn, cotton, in green
- Yarn C **(4 MEDIUM)**: 342yd/312m of Medium weight yarn, cotton, in dark pink
- Size E/4 (3.5mm) crochet hook OR SIZE TO OBTAIN GAUGE
- Scissors

GAUGE

- With Yarn A, 15 sts and 4 rows = 4"/10cm in [tr, ch 2] patt

TECHNIQUES

- Weaving ropes into foundation net (page 13)

instructions

FOUNDATION NET

With Yarn A, ch 188.

Row 1: Sc into 2nd ch from hook and in each of next rem chs—187 sc.

Row 2: Ch 6, tr in 4th sc from hook; *ch 2, sk next 2 sc, tr in next sc. Rep from * 61 times—62 tr and 62 ch-2 spaces.

Rows 3–83: Ch 6, tr in 1st tr from hook; *ch 2, tr in next tr. Rep from * 61 times—62 tr and 62 ch-2 spaces.

Row 84: Ch 1, sc in 1st tr, 2 sc in 1st ch-2 space; *sc in next tr, 2 sc in next ch-2 space.

Rep from * 61 times. End with sc in 4th ch of ch-4 of prev row—187 sc. Fasten off.

Foundation net is 62 'st' squares wide and 82 'row' squares long.

CROCHETING EDGES

Rnd 1: With RS of foundation net facing, bottom to your right, and Yarn A, insert hook in rightmost st at one edge, ch 1, 3 sc in same st, work along one side from bottom to top and 4 sc in each of next 82 dc spaces, 3 sc in corner st, sc in each of next sc along top, 3 sc in corner st, work along other side from top to bottom and 4 sc in each of next 82 dc spaces, 3 sc in corner st, sc in each of next ch of foundation chs along bottom. Join with sl st in 1st sc.

Rnd 2: Ch 1, sc in same sc as joining, 2 sc in next sc, sc in each of next sc along one side, 3 sc in corner sc, sc in each of next sc along top, 3 sc in corner sc, sc in each of next sc along other side, 3 sc in corner sc, sc in each of next sc along bottom. Join with sl st in 1st sc. Fasten off.

CROCHETING AND WEAVING ROPES INTO FOUNDATION NET

(Make 8)

With Yarn B, ch 2, and leave lp on hook. With RS of foundation net facing and bottom close to you, insert hook from RS to WS in bottom crocheted edge sc of foundation net, below middle of 7th (14th, 21st, 28th, 35th, 42nd, 49th, 56th) 'st' square, and work 2 overlay chs in each next 'sc' row; cont and ch 328 for rope. Leave untied large lp for later use, and cut yarn, leaving a 5"/12.5cm tail.

Weave rope in and out of each square along length of foundation net.

Insert hook in large lp, tighten lp, and insert hook in middle top of corresponding last 'row' square at top of foundation net, and work 2 overlay chs in each next 'sc' row. Ch 2, cut yarn and tie. Leave a 1½"/4cm tail at both ends.

(Make 18)

Follow same instructions as above using Yarn C, and inserting hook in bottom crocheted edge sc of foundation net, below middle of 3rd (4th, 10th, 11th, 17th, 18th, 24th, 25th, 31st, 32nd, 38th, 39th, 45th, 46th, 52nd, 53rd, 59th, 60th) 'st' square.

(Make 12)

With Yarn B, ch 2, and leave lp on hook. With RS of foundation net facing and bottom to your right, insert hook from RS to WS in closest side of crocheted edge sc of foundation net, below middle of 3rd (10th, 17th, 24th, 31st, 38th , 45th, 52nd, 59th, 66th, 73rd, 80th) 'row' square, and work 1 overlay ch in next 'sc' row; cont and ch 186 for rope. Leave untied large lp for later use, and cut yarn, leaving 5"/12.5cm tail.

Weave rope in and out of each square along width of foundation net, always over lengthwise ropes.

Insert hook in large lp, tighten lp, and insert hook in top middle of corresponding last 'st' square at farthest side of foundation net, and work 1 overlay ch in next 'sc' row. Ch 2, cut yarn and tie. Leave a 1½"/4cm tail at both ends.

this project was crocheted with

(A) 9 balls of Bernat Cottontots, 100% cotton, medium weight, approx 3.50oz/100g = 171yd/156m per ball, color 90012

(B) 2 balls of Bernat Cottontots, 100% cotton, medium weight, approx 3.50oz/100g = 171yd/156m per ball, color 90235

(C) 2 balls of Bernat Cottontots, 100% cotton, medium weight, approx 3.50oz/100g = 171yd/156m per ball, color 90531

From top to bottom: Garden Cushion Cover (opposite page), Wavy Landscape Cushion Cover (page 30)

garden cushion cover

This cushion cover is made entirely of bamboo wool, giving it a pleasantly touchable texture. Red, blue, green, and rust colored yarns are crocheted into rows like those found in a garden. A different composition of colors on each side results in a single cover that creates two effects.

EXPERIENCE LEVEL

■■■) Intermediate

FINISHED MEASUREMENTS

- 15"/38cm x 14"/35.5cm

MATERIALS AND TOOLS

- Yarn A **(4)**: 174yd /160m of Medium weight yarn, bamboo/wool, in deep red
- Yarn B **(4)**: 87yd /80m of Medium weight yarn, bamboo/wool, in rust
- Yarn C **(4)**: 87yd /80m of Medium weight yarn, bamboo/wool, in dark blue
- Yarn D **(4)**: 174yd /160m of Medium weight yarn, bamboo/wool, in bright green
- Size E/4 (3.5mm) crochet hook OR SIZE TO OBTAIN GAUGE
- One zipper, 10"/25.5cm long, deep red
- Straight pins
- Sewing needle and thread
- Scissors
- Cushion, 14"/35.6cm x 14"/35.6cm

GAUGE

- With Yarn A, 11 sts and 10 rows = 2"/5cm in sc

SPECIAL STITCHES

- Puff Stitch (page 11)

instructions

FRONT AND BACK

(Make 2)

With Yarn A (Yarn D), ch 64.

Row 1: Sc into 2nd ch from hook and in each of next rem chs—63 sc. Cut yarn.

Row 2: Join Yarn B, ch 1, sc into 1st sc from hook and in each of next rem sc—63 sc.

Cut yarn.

Row 3: Join Yarn C, ch 1, sc in 1st sc from hook and in each of next 2 sc; *Puff st in next sc, sc in each of next 3 sc. Rep from * 15 times—15 Puff sts. Cut yarn.

Row 4: Join Yarn B, ch 1, sc in 1st sc from hook and in each of next 2 sc; *sc in Puff st, sc in each of next 3 sc. Rep from * 15 times—63 sc. Cut yarn.

Row 5: Join Yarn A (Yarn D), ch 1, sc into 1st sc from hook and in each of next rem sc—63 sc.

Row 6: Ch 4, dc in 3rd sc from hook; *ch 1, sk next sc, dc in next sc. Rep from * 30 times—31 dc.

Row 7: Ch 1, sc in 1st dc of prev row, sc in next ch-1 space; *sc in next dc, sc in next ch-1 space. Rep from * 30 times. End with sc in 3rd ch of ch-4 of prev row—63 sc. Cut yarn.

Row 8: Rep row 2.

Row 9: Join Yarn D (Yarn A), ch 1, sc in 1st sc from hook and in each of next 2 sc; *Puff st in next sc, sc in each of next 3 sc. Rep from * 15 times—15 Puff sts. Cut yarn.

Row 10: Rep row 4.

Rows 11–13: Rep rows 5–7.

Row 14: Rep row 2.

Row 15: Rep row 3.

Row 16: Rep row 4.

Rows 17–19: Rep rows 5–7.

Rows 20–55: Rep rows 2–19, twice.

Rows 56–70: Rep rows 2–16.

Row 71: Rep row 5.

Rnd 72: Rep row 5. Cont with 3 sc in the corner. Work along one side, from top to bottom, and sc in each 'sc' row, and 2 sc in dc spaces (ch-4 spaces); 3 sc in next corner; cont along bottom, and sc in each ch of foundation chs; 3 sc in next corner; work along other side, from bottom to top, and sc in each 'sc' row and 2 sc in dc spaces (ch-4 spaces); 3 sc in next corner. Join with sl st in 1st sc.

Rnd 73: Ch 5, (dc, ch 1) all in each of next sc along top; (dc, ch 1) twice, all in corner sc; (dc, ch 1) all in each of next sc along one side; (dc, ch 1) twice, all in next corner sc; (dc, ch 1) all in each of next sc along bottom; (dc, ch 1) twice, all in next corner sc; (dc, ch 1) all in each of next sc along other side; (dc, ch 1) twice, all in next corner sc. Join with sl st in 4th ch of beg ch-5.

Rnd 74: Ch 1, sc in same st as joining, sc in 1st ch-1 space; *(sc in next dc, sc in next ch-1 space). Rep from * all around. Join with sl st in 1st sc. Fasten off.

ATTACHING BACK TO FRONT

Note: The terms back, front, top and sides refer to the crocheted piece, and not the finished item.

Place front and back with WS tog.

With RS of front facing, bottom to your right, and Yarn B, insert hook 2½"/6.5cm right from top, in edge sc at one side of front, and in corresponding sc of back, ch 1, sc in same pair of sts; sc in each of next rem pairs along front and back of one side, top, other side, bottom and one side again, until you are 2½"/6.5cm left from bottom.

Cont to work around front to form an opening for zipper, and sc in front lps only in each of next rem sc along 10"/25.5cm of one side of front. Turn and cont to work around back, and sc in front lps only in each of next rem sc along 10"/25.5cm of one side of back. Join with sl st in 1st sc of opening. Fasten off.

FAUX ROUND

With RS of front facing, bottom to your right, and Yarn B, insert hook in unused lp of 1st sc of opening, ch 1, sc in same unused lp and in each of next rem lps along front opening. Turn and cont to work and sc in each of next rem lps along back opening. Join with sl st in 1st sc of faux round. Fasten off.

ATTACHING ZIPPER

Place leftmost end of zipper at leftmost end of opening, and draw zipper to rightmost side along and behind faux rnd. Pin one side, then open zipper and pin other side. Sew on with backstitch.

this project was crocheted with

(A) 2 balls of Red Heart Eco-Ways Bamboo Wool, medium weight, 55%bamboo/45% wool, approx 1.75oz/50g = 87yd /80m per ball, color 3920

(B) 1 ball of Red Heart Eco-Ways Bamboo Wool, medium weight, 55%bamboo/45% wool, approx 1.75oz/50g = 87yd/80m per ball, color 3340

(C) 1 ball of Red Heart Eco-Ways Bamboo Wool, medium weight, 55%bamboo/45% wool, approx 1.75oz/50g = 87yd/80m per ball, color 3845

(D) 2 balls of Red Heart Eco-Ways Bamboo Wool, medium weight, 55%bamboo/45% wool, approx 1.75oz/50g = 87yd/80m per ball, color 3650

wavy landscape cushion cover

The pattern on this cushion cover resembles rows of planted vegetables on a windy day, as the wind blows them into waves. Made with bamboo wool, the cushion cover is as nice to touch as it is to look at.

EXPERIENCE LEVEL

■■■□ Intermediate

FINISHED MEASUREMENTS

- 14"/35.5cm x 14"/35.5cm

MATERIALS AND TOOLS

- Yarn A  : 174yd /160m of Medium weight yarn, bamboo/wool, in dark blue
- Yarn B  : 87yd /80m of Medium weight yarn, bamboo/wool, in rust
- Yarn C  : 87yd /80m of Medium weight yarn, bamboo/wool, in bright green
- Yarn D  : 174yd /160m of Medium weight yarn, bamboo/wool, in deep red
- Size E/4 (3.5mm) crochet hook OR SIZE TO OBTAIN GAUGE
- One zipper, 10"/25.5cm long, deep red
- Straight pins
- Sewing needle and thread
- Scissors
- Cushion, 14"/35.6cm x 14"/35.6cm

GAUGE

- With Yarn A, 9 sts and 6 rows = 2"/5cm in hdc

WAVE PATTERN

Pattern:

Row 1: Hdc in each of next 2 hdc, sc in each of next 3 dc, hdc in each of next 2 hdc, dc in each of next 3 sc

Row 2: Hdc in each of next 2 hdc, dc in each of next 3 sc, hdc in each of next 2 hdc, sc in each of next 3 dc

instructions

Note: Cut yarn when necessary, leaving a 1½"/4cm tail for later use.

FRONT AND BACK (Make 2)

With Yarn A (Yarn B), ch 64.

Row 1: Sc in 2nd ch of foundation chs, and in each of next 2 chs, hdc in each of next 2 chs, dc in each of next 3 chs, hdc in each of next 2 chs, sc in each of next 3 chs; *hdc in each of next 2 chs, dc in each of next 3 chs, hdc in each of next 2 chs, sc in each of next 3 chs. Rep from * 5 times. Cut yarn.

WAVE PATTERN

Row 2: Join Yarn B (Yarn C), ch 3, dc in 1st sc from hook and in each of next 2 sc, hdc in each of next 2 hdc, sc in each of next 3 dc, hdc in each of next 2 hdc, dc in each of next 3 sc; *hdc in each of next 2 hdc, sc in each of next 3 dc, hdc in each of next 2 hdc, dc in each of next 3 sc. Rep from * 5 times. Cut yarn.

Row 3: Join Yarn C (Yarn B), ch 1, sc in 1st dc from hook and in each of next 2 dc, hdc in each of next 2 hdc, dc in each of next 3 sc, hdc in each of next 2 hdc, sc in each of next 3 dc; *hdc in each of next 2 hdc, dc in each of next 3 sc, hdc in each of next 2 hdc, sc in each of next 3 dc. Rep from * 5 times. Cut yarn.

Row 4: Join Yarn D, ch 1, sc in 1st sc from hook and in each of next rem sts. Cut yarn.

Row 5: Join Yarn C (Yarn B), ch 3, dc in 1st sc from hook and in each of next 2 sc, hdc in each of next 2 sc, sc in each of next 3 sc, hdc in each of next 2 sc, dc in each of next 3 sc; *hdc in each of next 2 sc, sc in each of next 3 sc, hdc in each of next 2 sc, dc in each of next 3 sc. Rep from * 5 times. Cut yarn.

Row 6: Join Yarn B (Yarn C) and rep row 3.

Row 7: Join Yarn A (Yarn B) and rep row 2.

Row 8: Join Yarn D, ch 1, sc in 1st dc from hook and in each of next rem sts. Cut yarn.

Row 9: Join Yarn A (Yarn B), ch 1, sc in 1st sc from hook and in each of next 2 sc, hdc in each of next 2 sc, dc in each of next 3 sc, hdc in each of next 2 sc, sc in each of next 3 sc; *hdc in each of next 2 sc, dc in each of next 3 sc, hdc in each of next 2 sc, sc in each of next 3 sc. Rep from * 5 times. Cut yarn.

Rows 10–15: Rep rows 2–7.

Rows 16–55: Rep rows 8–15, 5 more times.

Row 56: Don't cut yarn. Rep row 8. Cont with 3 sc in the corner. Work along one side, from top to bottom, and sc in each edge sc (ch-1 spaces), and 2 sc in each edge dc (ch-4 spaces); 3 sc in next corner; cont along bottom, and sc in each ch of foundation chs; 3 sc in next corner; work along other side, from bottom to top, and sc in each edge sc (ch-1 spaces), and 2 sc in each edge dc (ch-4 spaces); 3 sc in next corner. Join with sl st in 1st sc.

ATTACHING BACK TO FRONT

Note: The terms back, front, top, bottom, and sides refer to the crocheted piece, and not the finished item.

Place front and back with WS tog.

With RS of front facing, bottom close to you, and Yarn D, insert hook 2½"/6.5cm right from left side in edge sc at top of front, and in corresponding sc of back, ch 1, sc in same pair of sts; sc in each of next rem pairs along front and back top, one side, bottom, other side, and top again, until you are 2½"/6.5cm left from right side.

Cont to work around front to form an opening for zipper, and sc in front lps only in each of next rem sc along 10"/25.5cm of front top. Turn and cont to work around back, and sc in front lps only in each of next rem sc along 10"/25.5cm of back top. Join with sl st in 1st sc of opening. Fasten off.

Bring yarn ends at each side to RS of front (back) while working, for later use.

FAUX ROUND

With Yarn D, follow same instructions as for Garden Cushion Cover (page 29).

FRINGES

With RS of front (back) facing, tie overhand knots double half-hitch knots along cushion sides with pairs of adjacent yarn ends. Trim yarn ends to ½"/1.3cm.

ATTACHING ZIPPER

Follow same instructions as for Garden Cushion Cover (page 29).

this project was crocheted with

(A) 2 balls of Red Heart Eco-Ways Bamboo Wool, medium weight, 55%bamboo/45% wool, approx 1.75oz/50g = 87yd /80m per ball, color 3845

(B) 1 ball of Red Heart Eco-Ways Bamboo Wool, medium weight, 55%bamboo/45% wool, approx 1.75oz/87yd, 50g/80m per ball, color 3340

(C) 1 ball of Red Heart Eco-Ways Bamboo Wool, medium weight, 55%bamboo/45% wool, approx 1.75oz/87yd, 50g/80m per ball, color 3650

(D) 2 balls of Red Heart Eco-Ways Bamboo Wool, medium weight, 55%bamboo/45% wool, approx 1.75oz/87yd, 50g/80m per ball, color 3920

fields of farms rug

This thick, room-warming rug looks like an aerial view of striped, rectangular, and square farmers' fields, in various colors and sizes. Durable and sturdy, the rug rolls into a tidy cylinder for easy storage during the summer. Though this project is technically easy, it requires a considerable amount of time and patience.

EXPERIENCE LEVEL

■■□□ Intermediate

FINISHED MEASUREMENTS

- 28"/121.9cm x 63"/161 m

MATERIALS AND TOOLS

- Yarn A (**6** SUPER BULKY): 306yds/280m of Bulky weight yarn, acrylic/wool, in dark gray
- Yarn B (**6** SUPER BULKY): 306yds/280m of Bulky weight yarn, acrylic/wool, in dark brown
- Yarn C (**6** SUPER BULKY): 306yds/280m of Bulky weight yarn, acrylic/wool, in greenish blue
- Yarn D (**6** SUPER BULKY): 459yds/420m of Bulky weight yarn, acrylic/wool, in brownish green
- Yarn E (**6** SUPER BULKY): 306yds/280m of Bulky weight yarn, acrylic/wool, in dark bluish green
- Yarn F (**6** SUPER BULKY): 153yds/140m of Bulky weight yarn, acrylic/wool, in deep orange
- Yarn G (**6** SUPER BULKY): 153yds/140m of Bulky weight yarn, acrylic/wool, in green
- Yarn H (**6** SUPER BULKY): 153yds/140m of Bulky weight yarn, acrylic/wool, in brownish orange

- Rope: 257yd/235m of Multi-ply jute twine, approx ³⁄₁₆"/5mm diameter, in natural beige
- Size H/7 (5mm) crochet hook OR SIZE TO OBTAIN GAUGE
- Scissors

GAUGE

- With Yarn A, 6 sts and 6 rows = 2"/5cm in sc over rope

TECHNIQUES

- Foundation row over rope (page 15)
- Single crochet over rope (page 16)

attention

This rug is made with natural fibers, so take care not to fold it, since folding can break the fibers.

instructions

PREPARATION

Cut rope into 182 pieces, 50½"/128cm each.

Note: Follow instructions below or see Fields of Farm Diagram on pages 126-127.

Foundation row: With Yarn A, starting 1½"/4cm left from one end of one rope piece, ch 1 over rope, 142 sc along and over rope. Distribute stitches, so you have 1½"/4cm tail of rope at end of row.

Use 1 piece of rope for each of next 181 rows. Start each row 1½"/4cm left from one end of rope, and finish leaving a 1½"/4cm tail of rope at other end.

Note: As the size of the carpet increases, roll crocheted part to make it easier to work.

Row 1–2: Ch 1 over rope, sc over rope in 1st sc from hook and in each of next rem sc—142 sc.

Row 3: *(With 1st ball of Yarn A, ch 1 over rope, sc over rope in 1st sc from hook and in each of next 4 sc)*, join Yarn B, sc over rope in each of next 90 sc, join Yarn C, sc over rope in each of next 42 sc, join 2nd ball of Yarn A, sc over rope in each of next 5 sc.

Row 4: **(With 2nd ball of Yarn A, ch 1 over rope, sc over rope in 1st sc from hook and in each of next 4 sc)**, join Yarn C, sc over rope in each of next 42 sc, join Yarn B, sc over rope in each of next 90 sc, with 1st ball of Yarn A, sc over rope in each of next 5 sc.

Note: In working rows 5-181, * means to repeat from * to * on row 3 once for first 5 sts; ** means to repeat from ** to ** on row 4 once for first 5 sts; numbers after yarns mean quantity of sc over rope made in each sc of previous row with specified yarn. Cut and join yarns as required.

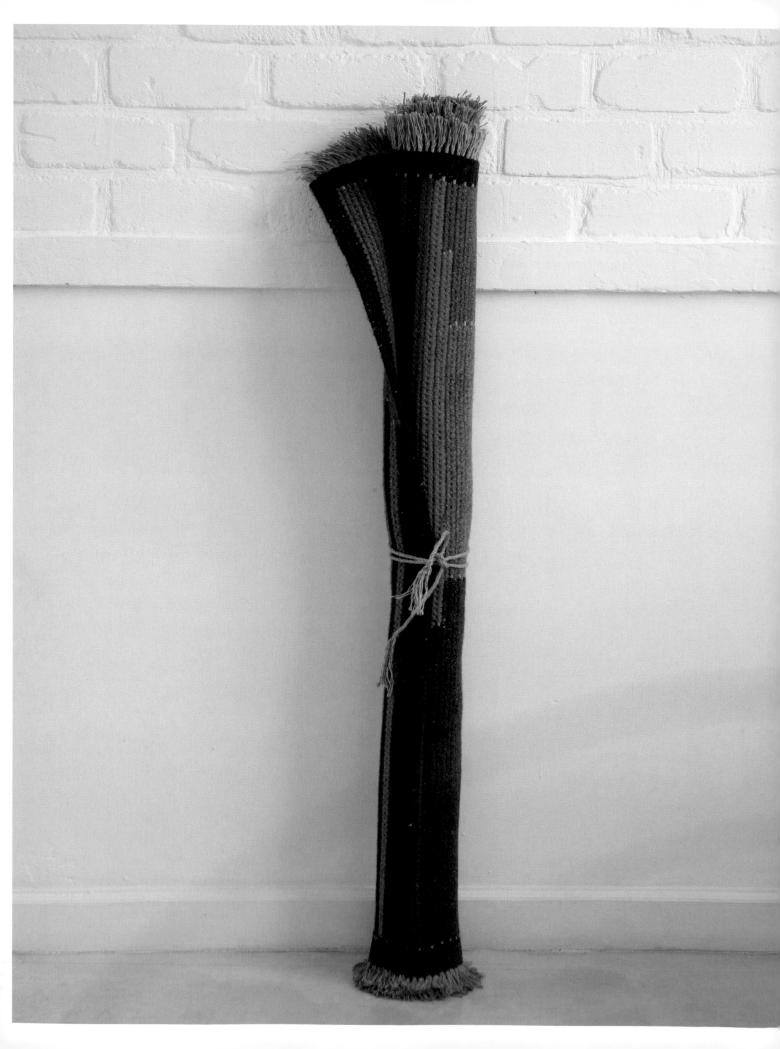

Row 5: *; Yarn D: 90; Yarn C: 42; 2nd ball of Yarn A: 5.

Row 6: **; Yarn C: 42; Yarn D: 90; 1st ball of Yarn A: 5.

Row 7: 1st ball of Yarn A: 5; Yarn B: 94; Yarn C: 38; 2nd ball of Yarn A: 5.

Row 8: **; Yarn C: 38; Yarn B: 94; 1st ball of Yarn A: 5.

Row 9: *; Yarn D: 94; Yarn C: 38; 2nd ball of Yarn A: 5.

Row 10: **; Yarn C: 38; Yarn D: 94; 1st ball of Yarn A: 5.

Rows 11–14: Rep rows 7–10.

Row 15: *; Yarn B: 106; Yarn C: 26; 2nd ball of Yarn A: 5.

Row 16: **; Yarn C: 26; Yarn B: 106; 1st ball of Yarn A: 5.

Row 17: *; Yarn D: 106; Yarn C: 26; 2nd ball of Yarn A: 5.

Row 18: **; Yarn C: 26; Yarn D: 106, 1st ball of Yarn A: 5.

Row 19: *; Yarn B: 60; Yarn D: 46; Yarn C: 26; 2nd ball of Yarn A: 5.

Row 20: **; Yarn C: 26; Yarn D: 46; Yarn B: 60; 2nd ball of Yarn A: 5.

Rows 21–24: Rep rows 17–20.

Row 25: *; Yarn E: 64; Yarn D: 42; Yarn C: 26; 2nd ball of Yarn A: 5.

Row 26: **; Yarn C: 26; Yarn D: 42; Yarn E: 64; 2nd ball of Yarn A: 5.

Rows 27–28: Rep rows 25–26.

Row 29: *; Yarn E: 64; Yarn D: 44; Yarn C: 24; 2nd ball of Yarn A: 5.

Row 30: **; Yarn C: 24; Yarn D: 44; Yarn E: 64; 2nd ball of Yarn A: 5.

Rows 31–38: Rep rows 29–30, 4 times.

Row 39: *; Yarn E: 56; Yarn G: 64; Yarn C: 12; 2nd ball of Yarn A: 5.

Row 40: **; Yarn C: 12; Yarn G: 64; Yarn E: 56; 2nd ball of Yarn A: 5.

Row 41: *; Yarn F: 66; Yarn G: 66; 2nd ball of Yarn A: 5.

Row 42: **; Yarn G: 66; Yarn F: 66; 1st ball of Yarn A: 5.

Row 43: *; Yarn F: 132; 2nd ball of Yarn A: 5.

Row 44: **; Yarn F: 132; 1st ball of Yarn A: 5.

Row 45: *; Yarn B: 132; 2nd ball of Yarn A: 5.

Row 46: **; Yarn B: 132; 1st ball of Yarn A: 5.

Rows 47–50: Rep rows 43–46.

Rows 51–52: Rep rows 43–44.

Row 53: *; Yarn B: 78; Yarn F: 54; 2nd ball of Yarn A: 5.

Row 54: **; Yarn F: 54; Yarn B: 78; 1st ball of Yarn A: 5.

Row 55: *; Yarn F: 82; Yarn G: 50; 2nd ball of Yarn A: 5.

Row 56: **; Yarn G: 50; Yarn F: 82; 1st ball of Yarn A: 5.

Row 57: *; Yarn F: 26; Yarn E: 62; Yarn G: 44; 2nd ball of Yarn A: 5.

Row 58: **; Yarn G: 44; Yarn E: 62; Yarn F: 26; 2nd ball of Yarn A: 5.

Row 59: *; Yarn F: 24; Yarn E: 54; Yarn G: 54; 2nd ball of Yarn A: 5.

Row 60: **; Yarn G: 54; Yarn E: 54; Yarn F: 24; 2nd ball of Yarn A: 5.

Row 61: *; Yarn E: 62; Yarn C: 36; Yarn G: 34; 2nd ball of Yarn A: 5.

Row 62: **; Yarn G: 34; Yarn C: 36; Yarn E: 62; 2nd ball of Yarn A: 5.

Rows 63–64: Rep rows 61–62.

Row 65: *; Yarn E: 62; Yarn C: 70; 2nd ball of Yarn A: 5.

Row 66: **; Yarn C: 70; Yarn E: 62; 1st ball of Yarn A.

Row 67: *; Yarn E: 62; Yarn G: 70; 2nd ball of Yarn A: 5.

Row 68: **; Yarn G: 70; Yarn E: 62; 1st ball of Yarn A: 5.

Rows 69–70: Rep rows 65–66.

Row 71: *; Yarn E: 36; Yarn B: 26; Yarn G: 70; 2nd ball of Yarn A: 5.

Row 72: **; Yarn G: 70; Yarn B: 26; Yarn E: 36; 2nd ball of Yarn A: 5.

Row 73: *; Yarn E: 36; Yarn B: 26; Yarn C: 70; 2nd ball of Yarn A: 5.

Row 74: **; Yarn C: 70; Yarn B: 26; Yarn E: 36; 2nd ball of Yarn A: 5.

Row 75: *; Yarn E: 36; Yarn B: 26; Yarn C: 42; Yarn D: 28; 2nd ball of Yarn A: 5.

Row 76: **; Yarn D: 28; Yarn C: 42; Yarn B: 26; Yarn E: 36; 2nd ball of Yarn A: 5.

Row 77: *; 1st ball of Yarn D: 40; Yarn B: 22; Yarn C: 26; 2nd ball of Yarn D: 44; 2nd ball of Yarn A: 5.

Row 78: **; 2nd ball of Yarn D: 44; Yarn C: 26; Yarn B: 22; 1st ball of Yarn D: 40; 2nd ball of Yarn A: 5.

Row 79: *; 1st ball of Yarn D: 40; Yarn B: 22; 2nd ball of Yarn D: 70; 2nd ball of Yarn A: 5.

Row 80: **; 2nd ball of Yarn D: 70; Yarn B: 22; 1st ball of Yarn D: 40; 2nd ball of Yarn A: 5.

Row 81: *; 1st ball of Yarn D: 40; Yarn B: 92; 2nd ball of Yarn A: 5.

Row 82: **; Yarn B: 92; 1st ball of Yarn D: 40; 2nd ball of Yarn A: 5.

Rows 83–84: Rep rows 79–80.

Row 85: *; 1st ball of Yarn D: 22; Yarn C: 20; Yarn B: 90; 2nd ball of Yarn A: 5.

Row 86: **; Yarn B: 90; Yarn C: 20; 1st ball of Yarn D: 22; 2nd ball of Yarn A: 5.

Row 87: *; 1st ball of Yarn D: 22; Yarn C: 20; Yarn B: 24; 2nd ball of Yarn D: 66; 2nd ball of Yarn A: 5.

Row 88: **; 2nd ball of Yarn D: 66; Yarn B: 24; Yarn C: 20; 1st ball of Yarn D: 22; 2nd ball of Yarn A: 5.

Rows 89–96: Rep rows 85–88, twice.

Rows 97–98: Rep rows 85–86.

Row 99: *; 1st ball of Yarn D: 22; Yarn C: 24; Yarn B: 24; 2nd ball of Yarn D: 62; 2nd ball of Yarn A: 5.

Row 100: **; 2nd ball of Yarn D: 62; Yarn B: 24; Yarn C: 24; 1st ball of Yarn D: 22; 2nd ball of Yarn A: 5.

Row 101: *; 1st ball of Yarn D: 22; Yarn C: 24; Yarn B: 86; 2nd ball of Yarn A: 5.

Row 102: **; Yarn B: 86; Yarn C: 24; 1st ball of Yarn D: 22; 2nd ball of Yarn A: 5.

Rows 103–104: Rep rows 99–100.

Row 105: *; Yarn D: 22; Yarn C: 40; Yarn B: 70; 2nd ball of Yarn A: 5.

Row 106: **; Yarn B: 70; Yarn C: 40; Yarn D: 22; 2nd ball of Yarn A: 5.

Row 107: *; Yarn D: 22; Yarn C: 40; Yarn B: 18; Yarn H: 52; 2nd ball of Yarn A: 5.

Row 108: **; Yarn H: 52; Yarn B: 18; Yarn C: 40; Yarn D: 22; 2nd ball of Yarn A: 5.

Row 109: *; Yarn G: 34; Yarn C: 28; Yarn B: 18; Yarn H: 52; 2nd ball of Yarn A: 5.

Row 110: **; Yarn H: 52; Yarn B: 18; Yarn C: 28; Yarn G: 34; 2nd ball of Yarn A: 5.

Rows 111–112: Rep rows 109–110.

Row 113: *; Yarn G: 38; Yarn C: 28; Yarn H: 66; 2nd ball of Yarn A: 5.

Row 114: **; Yarn H: 66; Yarn C: 28; Yarn G: 38; 2nd ball of Yarn A: 5.

Row 115: *; Yarn G: 66; Yarn H: 66; 2nd ball of Yarn A: 5.

Row 116: **; Yarn H: 66; Yarn G: 66; 2nd ball of Yarn A: 5.

Row 117: *; Yarn C: 66; Yarn E: 66; 2nd ball of Yarn A: 5.

Row 118: **; Yarn E: 66; Yarn C: 66; 2nd ball of Yarn A: 5.

Row 119: *; Yarn G: 66; Yarn E: 66; 2nd ball of Yarn A: 5.

Row 120: **; Yarn E: 66; Yarn G: 66; 2nd ball of Yarn A: 5.

Rows 121–122: Rep rows 117–118.

Row 123: *; Yarn G: 38; Yarn D: 40; Yarn E: 54; 2nd ball of Yarn A: 5.

Row 124: **; Yarn E: 54; Yarn D: 40; Yarn G: 38; 2nd ball of Yarn A: 5.

Row 125: *; Yarn C: 38; Yarn D: 40; Yarn E: 54; 2nd ball of Yarn A: 5.

Row 126: **; Yarn E: 54; Yarn D: 40; Yarn C: 38; 2nd ball of Yarn A: 5.

Rows 127–132: Rep rows 123–124, 3 times.

Row 133: *; Yarn G: 42; Yarn D: 40; Yarn E: 50; 2nd ball of Yarn A: 5.

Row 134: **; Yarn E: 50; Yarn D: 40; Yarn G: 42; 2nd ball of Yarn A: 5.

Rows 135–136: Rep rows 133–134.

Row 137: *; Yarn F: 42; Yarn D: 40; Yarn E: 50; 2nd ball of Yarn A: 5.

Row 138: **; Yarn E: 50; Yarn D: 40; Yarn F: 42; 2nd ball of Yarn A: 5.

Row 139: *; Yarn F: 48; Yarn D: 44; Yarn E: 40; 2nd ball of Yarn A: 5.

Row 140: **; Yarn E: 40; Yarn D: 44; Yarn F: 48; 2nd ball of Yarn A: 5.

Rows 141–142: Rep rows 139–140.

Row 143: *; Yarn F: 48; Yarn D: 44; Yarn H: 40; 2nd ball of Yarn A: 5.

Row 144: **; Yarn H: 40; Yarn D: 44; Yarn F: 48; 2nd ball of Yarn A: 5.

Rows 145–148: Rep rows 143–144, twice.

Row 149: *; Yarn F: 52; Yarn D: 44; Yarn H: 36; 2nd ball of Yarn A: 5.

Row 150: **; Yarn H: 36; Yarn D: 44; Yarn F: 52; 2nd ball of Yarn A: 5.

Rows 151–154: Rep rows 149–150, twice.

Row 155: *; Yarn G: 52; Yarn B: 80; 2nd ball of Yarn A: 5.

Row 156: **; Yarn B: 80; Yarn G: 52; 2nd ball of Yarn A: 5.

Row 157: *; Yarn G: 52; Yarn D: 80; 2nd ball of Yarn A: 5.

Row 158: **; Yarn D: 80; Yarn G: 52; 2nd ball of Yarn A: 5.

Rows 159–160: Rep rows 155–156.

Row 161: *; Yarn G: 58; Yarn D: 74; 2nd ball of Yarn A: 5.

Row 162: **; Yarn D: 74; Yarn G: 58; 2nd ball of Yarn A: 5.

Row 163: *; Yarn C: 58; Yarn B: 74; 2nd ball of Yarn A: 5.

Row 164: **; Yarn B: 74; Yarn C: 58; 2nd ball of Yarn A: 5.

Row 165: *; Yarn C: 58; Yarn D: 74; 2nd ball of Yarn A: 5.

Row 166: **; Yarn D: 74; Yarn C: 58; 2nd ball of Yarn A: 5.

Rows 167–174: Rep rows 163–166, twice.

Row 175: *; Yarn C: 62; Yarn B: 70; 2nd ball of Yarn A: 5.

Row 176: **; Yarn B: 70; Yarn C: 62; 2nd ball of Yarn A: 5.

Row 177: *; Yarn C: 62; Yarn D: 70; 2nd ball of Yarn A: 5.

Row 178: **; Yarn D: 70; Yarn C: 62; 2nd ball of Yarn A: 5.

Rows 179–181: Yarn: 142.

Fasten off. Fray ends of each piece of rope.

this project was crocheted with

(A) 2 balls of Lion Wool-Ease Chunky Yarn, 80% acrylic/20% wool, bulky weight, approx 5oz/140g = 153yrds/140m per ball, color 630-152

(B) 2 balls of Lion Wool-Ease Chunky Yarn, 80% acrylic/20% wool, bulky weight, approx 5oz/140g = 153yrds/140m per ball, color 630-127

(C) 2 balls of Lion Wool-Ease Chunky Yarn, 80% acrylic/20% wool, bulky weight, approx 5oz/140g = 153yrds/140m per ball, color 630-178

(D) 3 balls of Lion Wool-Ease Chunky Yarn, 80% acrylic/20% wool, bulky weight, approx 5oz/140g = 153yrds/140m per ball, color 630 173

(E) 2 balls of Lion Wool-Ease Chunky Yarn, 80% acrylic/20% wool, bulky weight, approx 5oz/140g = 153yrds/140m per ball, color 630-180

(F) 1 ball of Lion Wool-Ease Chunky Yarn, 80% acrylic/20% wool, bulky weight, approx 5oz/140g = 153yrds/140m per ball, color 630-186

(G) 1 ball of Lion Wool-Ease Chunky Yarn, 80% acrylic/20% wool, bulky weight, approx 5oz/140g = 153yrds/140m per ball, color 630-130

(H) 1 ball of Lion Wool-Ease Chunky Yarn, 80% acrylic/20% wool, bulky weight, approx 5oz/140g = 153yrds/140m per ball, color 630-135

(Rope) 3-ply jute twine, 100% jute, approx 3/16"/5mm diameter, in natural beige

strips of sprouts wall hanging

This impressive wall hanging features dozens of sprout-like strips, each of which is decorated with a handful of buds. The buds are arranged in several different manners, giving the impression that no two sprouts are the same—much as it is in nature.

EXPERIENCE LEVEL

■■■□ Intermediate

FINISHED MEASUREMENTS

- 49"/124.5cm wide x 44"/112cm long

MATERIALS AND TOOLS

- Yarn A : 555yd/507m of Worsted weight yarn, recycled cotton/acrylic/other fibers, in variegated green and white

- Yarn B **4**: 328yd/300m of Worsted weight yarn, organic cotton, in cream

- Yarn C **4**: 82yd/75m of Worsted weight yarn, organic cotton, in light gray

- Size E/4 (3.5mm) crochet hook OR SIZE TO OBTAIN GAUGE

- Two 49"/124.5cm round steel rods, ⅛"/3mm diameter, or ½"/1.3cm shorter than width of frame

- Two ¾"/2cm wide x 51"/130 cm long pieces of bias tape, cream

- Stitch markers

- Scissors

- Sewing needle and matching thread

- Straight pins

- Three small ring-shaped picture hangers

GAUGE

- With Yarn B, 9 sts and 12 rows= 2"/5cm in sc

SPECIAL STITCHES

- Reverse single crochet stitch (reverse sc) (page 10)

- Bud: ch 4, sl st in 4th ch from hook (See Picot, page 10)

TECHNIQUES

- Attaching to frame (page 13)

instructions

CROCHETED RECTANGLE FRAME

With Yarn C, ch 842, join with sl st in 1st ch to form a ring.

Rnd 1: Ch 1, sc in same ch as joining and in each of next 841 chs, placing stitch markers on increase points (corners), while working. Join with sl st in 1st sc—842 sc.

Place stitch markers on: 201st sc, 421st sc, 622nd sc, 842nd sc. Cut yarn.

Rnd 2: Join Yarn B, ch 1, sc in same sc as joining and in each of next rem sc, making 3 sc in 201st sc, 421st sc, 622nd sc, 842nd sc. Join with sl st in 1st sc—850 sc.

Rnd 3: Ch 1, sc in same sc as joining and in each of next 849 sc, placing stitch markers on increase points (corners), while working. Join with sl st in 1st sc.

Place stitch markers on: 202nd sc, 424th sc, 627th sc, 849th sc.

Rnd 4: Ch 1, sc in same sc as joining and in each of next rem sc, making 3 sc in 202nd sc, 424th sc, 627th sc, 849th sc. Join with sl st in 1st sc—858 sc.

Rnd 5: Ch 1, sc in same sc as joining and in each of next 857 sc, placing stitch markers on increase points (corners), while working. Join with sl st in 1st sc.

Place stitch markers on: 203rd sc, 427th sc, 632nd sc, 856th sc.

Rnd 6: Ch 1, sc in same sc as joining and in each of next rem sc, making 3 sc in 203rd sc, 427th sc, 632nd sc, 856th sc. Join with sl st in 1st sc—866 sc.

Rnd 7: Working left to right, ch 1, reverse sc in same st as joining and in each of next rem sc—866 reverse sc. Join with sl st in joining st of prev rnd. Fasten off.

CROCHETING INNER RECTANGLE FRAME

Note: Inner bottom of crocheted rectangle frame is last 221 foundation chs.

With RS of rectangle frame facing, bottom to your left, and Yarn C, insert hook in leftmost unused lp of foundation chs at closest side. Working left to right, ch 1, reverse sc in same unused lp and in each of next 198 unused lps along closest side from bottom to top, sk next 2 unused lps, reverse sc in each of next 219 unused lps along top, sk next 2 unused lps, reverse sc in each of next 199 unused lps along other side from top to bottom. Fasten off.

GARDEN

Note: Plant grass and sprouts (see below) along inner bottom of rectangle frame, and connect each sprout to inner top of frame while working.

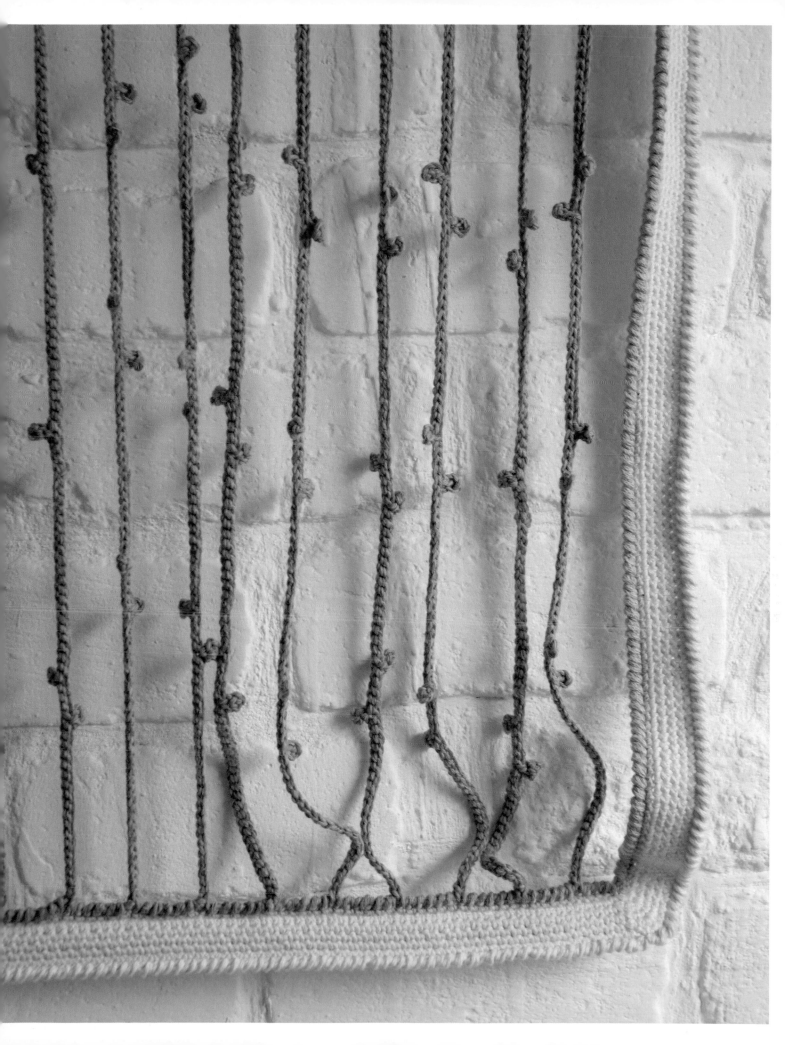

With RS of rectangle frame facing, bottom close to you and Yarn A, insert hook in leftmost unused lp of foundation chs at inner bottom of rectangle frame. Working left to right, ch 1, reverse sc in same unused lp and in each of next 4 unused lps along bottom, *make a sprout variation (see below); reverse sc in each of next 5 unused lps along bottom. Rep from * 36 times—36 sprouts and 185 reverse sc. Fasten off.

SPROUT VARIATIONS

Note: The sprouts grow in parallel columns, and each sprout consists of 2 rows. There are several possible variations for each sprout.

Row 1: With lp on hook, insert hook in next unused lp at inner bottom of rectangle frame, ch 20 (25, 30), bud (page 45), sl st in prev ch; *ch 25, bud, sl st in prev ch. Rep from * 7 times. Cont and ch 25 (20, 15). With lp on hook, insert hook behind reverse sc in corresponding lp of foundation chs at inner top of rectangle frame and overlay ch 1.

Note: There are buds on both rows of each sprout, so that the buds face more than one direction, as in nature. Buds in the 2nd row must be separated from buds in the 1st row by 5 sl sts. They may be placed either below or above the 1st row buds.

Row 2: With RS of rectangle frame facing and bottom away from you, sl st in 1st ch from hook and in each of next 19 or 29 (14 or 24, 9 or 19) chs, bud, sl st in prev ch; * sl st in each of next chs, until 5 chs are left before prev row bud, or until you are 5 chs after prev row bud, bud, sl st in prev ch. Rep from * 7 times. Cont and sl st in each of next 24 or 14 (29 or 19, 34 or 24) chs, sl st in same lp as at beg of row 1. Don't cut yarn.

ATTACHING BIAS TAPE

Note: If possible, use a sewing machine to sew on bias tape.

Make a 1"/2.5 fold at both ends of bias tape. Rep twice. With WS of frame facing, place bias tape along top (bottom) of frame, with folded ends downwards, and pin. Using whip stitch, sew on along edges of both long sides and one end. Insert metal rod, and sew up open end. Sew picture hangers on bias tape at top of frame, at both sides and center.

this project was crocheted with

(A) 3 balls of Lion Recycled Cotton, 72% Recycled Cotton, 24% Acrylic, 4% Other Fiber, Worsted weight, approx 3.5oz/100g = 185yd/169m, color 482-130

(B) 4 balls of Lion Organic Cotton Yarn, medium worsted weight, 100% organic cotton, approx 1.75oz/50g = 82yd/75m per ball, color 680-001

(C) 1 ball of Lion Organic Cotton Yarn, medium worsted weight, 100% organic cotton, approx 1.75oz/50g = 82yd/75m per ball, color 680-001

framed flowery fields

The three pieces in this project are like a collection of snapshots taken on a fresh spring day. Each field features a different combination of colors, evoking different scenes. Make a single piece or all three.

EXPERIENCE LEVEL

■■■ ◻ Intermediate

FINISHED MEASUREMENTS

- 5½"/14cm x 5½"/14cm

MATERIALS AND TOOLS

- Yarn A **MEDIUM 4**: 82yd/75m of Medium Worsted weight yarn, organic cotton, in light gray (light beige, dark beige)
- Yarn B **LACE 0**: 300yds/274m of Crochet thread, bamboo, in light green
- Yarn C **LACE 0**: 300yds/274m of Crochet thread, bamboo, in light blue (light blue, light yellow)
- Size E/4 (3.5mm) crochet hook OR SIZE TO OBTAIN GAUGE
- Size 7 (1.5mm) steel crochet hook OR SIZE TO OBTAIN GAUGE
- Deep frame with mat, white, 9" x 9" x 1¾" (23cm x 23cm x 4.5cm)
- Adhesive tape
- Scissors

GAUGE

- With Yarn A, 9 sts and 10 rows = 2"/5cm in sc

SPECIAL STITCHES

- Loop Stitch (page 11)
- Picot: Ch 3, sl st in 1st ch of ch-3 (page 10)

instructions

Field (for a set of three, make one of each color)

With Yarn A and E/4 (3.5mm) crochet hook, ch 26.

Row 1: Sc into 2nd ch from hook and in each of next rem chs—25 sc.

Rows 2–3: Ch 1, sc into 1st sc from hook and in each of next rem sc—25 sc.

Row 4: Ch 1, sc into 1st sc from hook and in each of next 2 sc. Loop st in next sc and in each of next 19 sc, sc in each of next rem 3 sc—6 sc and 19 Loop sts.

Row 5: Ch 1, sc into 1st sc from hook and in each of next 2 sc, sc in each of next 19 Loop sts, sc in each of next rem 3 sc—25 sc.

Rows 6–25: Rep rows 4–5, 10 times.

Rows 26–27: Ch 1, sc into 1st sc from hook and in each of next rem sc—25 sc.

Fasten off.

CORNFLOWER/BUTTERCUP
(plant 9, or as many as you like)

Stem

With RS of field facing, Yarn B and Size 7 (1.5mm) steel crochet hook, insert hook through sc st (btw Loop st rows) where you want to plant flower, pull yarn through, and ch 8. Cut yarn and tie bottom end. Don't hide tail of loose end (it will be stamen of finished flower).

Petals

With Yarn C and Size 7 (1.5mm) steel crochet hook, insert hook into 2nd ch at stem end, *picot, sc in same ch of stem. Rep from * twice in front lp of ch and once in back lp of same ch, with tail of Yarn B extending upwards. End with sl st in 1st ch from beg rnd. Fasten off. Trim tail to ¼"(0.6cm), and fray.

FRAMING

Place mat WS upwards, and place crocheted field on top, WS upwards. Tape field edges to mat with tape. Insert into frame.

this project was crocheted with

(A) 1 ball of Lion Organic Cotton Yarn, medium worsted weight, 100% organic cotton, approx 1.75oz/50g = 82yd/75m per ball, color 680-004 (680-002, 680-003)

(B) 1 ball of Aunt Lydia's Bamboo Crochet Thread, 100% bamboo, approx 2oz/59g = 300yds/274m per ball, color 0661

(C) 1 ball of Aunt Lydia's Bamboo Crochet Thread, 100% bamboo, approx 2oz/59g = 300yds/274m per ball, color 0810 (0810, 0240)

large luminous pod

This pod-shaped lampshade features hundreds of holes that allow light to gently dapple out. Flexible and malleable, its shape can be altered with ease.

EXPERIENCE LEVEL

■■■□ Intermediate

FINISHED MEASUREMENTS

- About 34"/86.5cm high

MATERIALS AND TOOLS

- Yarn A **(3 LIGHT)**: 516yd/472m of Light weight yarn, cotton/corn, in variegated light brown and white

- Yarn B **(3 LIGHT)**: 258yd/236m of Light weight yarn, cotton/corn, in variegated light green and white

- Yarn C **(2 FINE)**: 21.8yd/20m of Thin, 3-strand hemp yarn, in natural beige

- Rope: 65yd/60m of Multi-ply jute twine, approx ³⁄₁₆"/5mm diameter, in natural beige

- Size E/4 (3.5mm) crochet hook OR SIZE TO OBTAIN GAUGE

- Drum-shaped lampshade frame, 26"/66cm high x 4"/10cm (diameter at top) x 8½"/21.5cm (diameter at bottom)

- Basic standing lamp electricity kit (such as mason jar lamp kit)

- One piece of 18-gauge half-hard round steel wire, 16½"/41.9cm long

- Wire cutters

- Scissors

GAUGE

- With Yarn A, 9 sts and 3 rows = 2"/5cm in dc over rope, ch 2 above rope pattern

SPECIAL STITCHES

- Picot: Ch 3, sl st in 1st ch of ch-3 (page 10)

TECHNIQUES

- Foundation round over rope (page 15)

- Single crochet over rope (page 16)

- Chain above rope, single crochet over rope (page 16)

- Half double crochet over rope (page 17)

- Double crochet over rope (page 17)

attention

This lampshade is not intended to withstand high temperatures such as those generated by high-wattage incandescent light bulbs. Use a low-wattage, low heat-generating light bulb with this lampshade. Also, make sure the lampshade does not come in direct contact with the light bulb, or any other heat source.

This lampshade is made with natural fibers, so take care not to fold it, since this could cause the fibers to break.

instructions

LAMPSHADE

Foundation row: With free end of rope to your right and Yarn B, ch 1 over rope (leaving 36"/91.5cm rope tail for later use), 16 sc along and over rope.

Rnd 1: Curve foundation row into a ring, and carry rope and yarn above foundation row to connect ring by making sc over rope into 1st sc of foundation row. Curving rope around foundation row, sc over rope in each of next 15 sc—16 sc.

Note: Curve rope above each of next rounds, following instructions below.

Rnds 2–6: Sc over rope in each of next 16 sc.

Note: Curve rope above each of next rounds, making each next round wider than previous, and following instructions below.

Rnd 7: *Sc over rope in each of next 3 sc, 2 sc over rope in next sc. Rep from * 4 times—20 sc.

Rnds 8–9: Sc over rope in each of next 20 sc.

Rnd 10: *Sc over rope in each of next 4 sc, 2 sc over rope in next sc. Rep from * 4 times—24 sc.

Rnd 11: Sc over rope in each of next 24 sc.

Rnd 12: *Sc over rope in each of next 5 sc, 2 sc over rope in next sc. Rep from * 4 times—28 sc.

Rnd 13: *Sc over rope in each of next 6 sc, 2 sc over rope in next sc. Rep from * 4 times—32 sc.

Rnd 14: *Sc over rope in each of next 7 sc, 2 sc over rope in next sc. Rep from * 4 times—36 sc.

Rnd 15: *Sc over rope in each of next 8 sc, 2 sc over rope in next sc. Rep from * 4 times—40 sc.

Rnd 16: *Sc over rope in each of next 9 sc, 2 sc over rope in next sc. Rep from * 4 times—44 sc.

Rnd 17: *Sc over rope in each of next 10 sc, 2 sc over rope in next sc. Rep from * 4 times—48 sc.

Rnd 18: *Ch 2 above rope, sk next sc, sc over rope in next sc. Rep from * 24 times—24 sc and 24 ch-2 spaces.

Rnd 19: (Ch 2 above rope, sc over rope) all in each of next 24 ch-2 spaces.

Rnd 20: *(Ch 2 above rope, sc over rope) all in each of next 5 ch-2 spaces, (ch 2 above rope, sc over rope, ch 2 above rope, sc over rope) in next ch-2 space. Rep from * 4 times—28 sc and 28 ch-2 spaces.

Rnd 21: (Ch 2 above rope, sc over rope) all in each of next 28 ch-2 spaces.

Rnd 22: *(Ch 2 above rope, sc over rope) all in each of next 6 ch-2 spaces, (ch 2 above rope, sc over rope, ch 2 above rope, sc over rope) in next ch-2 space. Rep from * 4 times—32 sc and 32 ch-2 spaces.

Rnds 23–25: (Ch 2 above rope, sc over rope) all in each of next 32 ch-2 spaces.

Rnds 26–28: Join Yarn A and rep rnds 23–25.

Rnds 29–32: (Ch 2 above rope, hdc over rope) all in each of next 32 ch-2 spaces—32 hdc and 32 ch-2 spaces.

Rnds 33–38: (Ch 2 above rope, dc over rope) all in each of next 32 ch-2 spaces—32 dc and 32 ch-2 spaces.

Rnd 39: *(Ch 2 above rope, dc over rope) all in each of next 7 ch-2 spaces, (ch 2 above rope, dc over rope, ch 2 above rope, dc over rope) in next ch-2 space. Rep from * 4 times—36 dc and 36 ch-2 spaces.

Rnds 40–47: (Ch 2 above rope, dc over rope) all in each of next 36 ch-2 spaces.

Rnds 48–53: (Ch 2 above rope, hdc over rope) all in each of next 36 ch-2 spaces.

Rnd 54: *(Ch 2 above rope, sc over rope) all in each of next 8 ch-2 spaces, (ch 2 above rope, sc over rope, ch 2 above rope, sc over rope) in next ch-2 space. Rep from * 4 times—40 sc and 40 ch-2 spaces.

Rnds 55–62: (Ch 2 above rope, sc over rope) all in each of next 40 ch-2 spaces.

Rnds 63–68: (Ch 2 above rope, hdc over rope) all in each of

From left to right: Small Luminous Pod (page 55), Large Luminous Pod

next 40 ch-2 spaces—40 hdc and 40 ch-2 spaces.

Rnd 69: *(Ch 2 above rope, dc over rope) all in each of next 9 ch-2 spaces, (ch 2 above rope, dc over rope, ch 2 above rope, dc over rope) in next ch-2 space. Rep from * 4 times—44 dc and 44 ch-2 spaces.

Rnds 70–73: (Ch 2 above rope, dc over rope) all in each of next 44 ch-2 spaces.

Rnd 74: *(Ch 2 above rope, hdc over rope) all in each of next 10 ch-2 spaces, (ch 2 above rope, hdc over rope, ch 2 above rope, hdc over rope) in next ch-2 space. Rep from * 4 times—48 hdc and 48 ch-2 spaces.

Rnd 75: (Ch 2 above rope, sc over rope) all in each of next 48 ch-2 spaces—48 sc and 48 ch-2 spaces. Cut rope and fasten in place.

Rnd 76: *2 sc in next ch-2 space, sc in next sc. Rep from * 48 times. Join with sl st in 1st sc—144 sc.

Rnd 77: Picot, sk joining st, * sl st in next sc, picot, sk next sc. Rep from * 71 times. Join with sl st in joining st of prev rnd. Fasten off.

STEM

Make a fold in rope tail at top of cover, so that free end of tail extends 1"/2.5cm beyond other tail end. With one hand, hold folded rope, wire, and 3"/7.5cm of free end of Yarn C tog (ball of Yarn C is in other hand). Starting ½"/1.3cm down from top, wrap Yarn C tightly over folded rope, wire, and hemp yarn tail, then cont wrapping folded rope and wire all the way to bottom end. Tie an overhand knot at the end. Cut yarn. Hide rope and yarn tail inside cover.

Place lampshade over lamp frame, and place lamp frame over lamp electricity kit.

this project was crocheted with

(A) 4 balls of Bernat Cot'n Corn Natural Blends, 67%cotton/33%corn, lightweight, approx 2.1oz/60g = 129yd/118m per ball, color 19010

(B) 2 balls of Bernat Cot'n Corn Natural Blends, 67%cotton/33%corn, lightweight, approx 2.1oz/60g = 129yd/118m per ball, color 19244

(C): 1 spool of HempBasics, 100% hemp 3-strand yarn, approx 17.6oz/500g = 1800yd/ 1642m per spool

(Rope) 3-ply jute twine, 100% jute, approx ³⁄₁₆"/5mm diameter, in natural beige

small luminous pod

This lampshade, a smaller version of the lampshade on page 50, features different colors in the same earthy style. Both pieces are striking on their own, and make a distinct pair when positioned together, or in different corners of the same room.

EXPERIENCE LEVEL

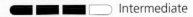 Intermediate

FINISHED MEASUREMENTS

- About 30"/76cm high

MATERIALS AND TOOLS

- Yarn A **SUPER BULKY 6**: 252yd/228m of Bulky weight yarn, bamboo/acrylic/polyester, in cream

- Yarn B **SUPER BULKY 6**: 126yd/114m of Bulky weight yarn, bamboo/acrylic/polyester, in light brown

- Yarn C **FINE 2**: 21.8yd/20m of Thin, 3-strand hemp yarn, in natural beige Rope: 65yd/60m of Multi-ply jute twine, approx 3/16"/5mm diameter, in natural beige

- Rope: 55yd/50m of Multi-ply jute twine, approx $^3/_{16}$"/5mm diameter, in natural beige

- Size E/4 (3.5mm) crochet hook OR SIZE TO OBTAIN GAUGE

- Drum-shaped lampshade frame, 22"/56cm high x 4"/10cm (diameter at top) x 8"/20.5cm (diameter at bottom)

- Basic standing lamp electricity kit (such as mason jar lamp kit)

- Scissors

GAUGE

- With Yarn A, 9 sts and 3 rows = 2"/5cm in dc over rope, ch 2 above rope pattern

SPECIAL STITCHES

- Picot: Ch 3, sl st in 1st ch of ch-3 (page 10)

TECHNIQUES

- Foundation round over rope (page 15)

- Single crochet over rope (page 16)

- Chain above rope, single crochet over rope (page 16)

- Half double crochet over rope (page 17)

- Double crochet over rope (page 17)

attention

This lampshade is not intended to withstand high temperatures such as those generated by high-wattage incandescent light bulbs. Use a low-wattage, low heat-generating light bulb with this lampshade. Also, make sure the lampshade does not come in direct contact with the light bulb, or any other heat source.

This lampshade is made with natural fibers, so take care not to fold it, since this could cause the fibers to break.

instructions

LAMPSHADE

Foundation row: With free end of rope to your right and Yarn B, ch 1 over rope (leaving 40"/101.6cm tail of rope for later use), 12 sc along and over rope.

Rnd 1: Curve foundation row into a ring, and carry rope and yarn above foundation row to connect ring by making sc over rope into 1st sc of foundation row. Curving rope around foundation row, sc over rope in each of next 11 sc—12 sc.

Note: Curve rope above each of next rounds, making each next round wider than previous, and following instructions below.

Rnd 2: *Sc over rope in each of next 2 sc, 2 sc over rope in next sc. Rep from * 4 times—16 sc.

Rnd 3: Rep rnd 2 of Large Luminous Pod (page 52)—16 sc.

Rnds 4–5: Rep rnds 7–8 of Large Luminous Pod (page 52)—20 sc.

Rnds 6–7: Rep rnds 10–11 of Large Luminous Pod (page 52)—24 sc.

Rnd 8: *Sc over rope in each of next 2 sc, 2 sc over rope in next sc. Rep from * 8 times—32 sc.

Rnd 9: *Sc over rope in each of next 3 sc, 2 sc over rope in next sc. Rep from * 8 times—40 sc. Cut yarn.

Rnd 10: Join Yarn A, *sc over rope in each of next 4 sc, 2 sc over rope in next sc. Rep from * 8 times—48 sc.

Rnd 11: Sc over rope in each of next 48 sc.

Rnds 12–13: With Yarn A, rep rnds 18–19 of Large Luminous Pod (page 52)—24 sc and 24 ch-2 spaces.

Rnds 14–17: (Ch 2 above rope, hdc over rope) all in each of next 24 ch-2 spaces—24 hdc and 24 ch-2 spaces.

Rnds 18–22: (Ch 2 above rope, dc over rope) all in each of next 24 ch-2 spaces—24 dc and 24 ch-2 spaces.

From left to right: Large Luminous Pod (page 50), Small Luminous Pod

Rnd 23: *(Ch 2 above rope, dc over rope) all in each of next 5 ch-2 spaces, (ch 2 above rope, dc over rope, ch 2 above rope, dc over rope) in next ch-2 space. Rep from * 4 times—28 dc and 28 ch-2 spaces.

Rnds 24–31: (Ch 2 above rope, dc over rope) all in each of next 28 ch-2 spaces.

Rnd 32: *(Ch 2 above rope, dc over rope) all in each of next 6 ch-2 spaces, (ch 2 above rope, dc over rope, ch 2 above rope, dc over rope) in next ch-2 space. Rep from * 4 times—32 dc and 32 ch-2 spaces.

Rnds 33–42: (Ch 2 above rope, dc over rope) all in each of next 32 ch-2 spaces.

Rnds 43–44: Rep rnds 39–40 of Large Luminous Pod (page 52)—36 dc and 36 ch-2 spaces. Cut yarn.

Rnds 45–53: Join Yarn B and rep rnd 48 of Large Luminous Pod (page 52)—36 hdc and 36 ch-2 spaces. Cut yarn.

Rnds 54–55: Join Yarn A and rep rnd 48 of Large Luminous Pod (page 52)—36 hdc and 36 ch-2 spaces.

Rnd 56: Rep rnd 54 of Large Luminous Pod (page 52)—40 sc and 40 ch-2 spaces. Cut rope and fasten in place.

Rnd 57: *2 sc in next ch-2 space, sc in next sc. Rep from * 40 times. Join with sl st in 1st sc—120 sc.

Rnd 58: Picot, sk joining st, * sl st in next sc, picot, sk next sc. Rep from * 59 times. Join with sl st in joining st of prev rnd. Fasten off.

STEM

Make a fold in rope tail at top of cover, so that free end of tail extends 1"/2.5cm beyond other tail end. With one hand, hold folded rope and 3"/7.5cm of free end of Yarn C tog (ball of Yarn C is in other hand). Starting ½"/1.3cm down from top, wrap Yarn C tightly over folded rope and hemp yarn tail, then cont wrapping folded rope all the way to bottom end. Tie an overhand knot at the end. Cut yarn. Hide rope and yarn tail inside cover.

Place lampshade over lamp frame, and place lamp frame over lamp electricity kit.

this project was crocheted with

(A) 4 balls of Bernat Bamboo Natural Blends, 86% bamboo/12% acrylic/2% polyester, bulky weight, approx 2.1oz/60g = 63yd/57m per ball, color 92008

(B) 2 ball of Bernat Bamboo Natural Blends, 86% bamboo/12% acrylic/2% polyester, bulky weight, approx 2.1oz/60g = 63yd/57m per ball, color 92011

(C) 1 spool of HempBasics, 100% hemp 3-strand yarn, approx 17.6oz/500g = 1800yd/ 1642m per spool

(Rope) 3-ply jute twine, 100% jute, approx ³⁄₁₆"/5mm diameter, in natural beige

sophisticated sweet sheep

Who says stuffed animals are just for kids. This adorable lamb can be placed in a child's room, but it can also be an elegant home accessory. With its creamy fur, black legs, and curious expression, it's a great piece for softening any room décor. The texture of this toy is reminiscent of a real lamb, making it eminently easy to pet.

EXPERIENCE LEVEL

■■■□ Intermediate

FINISHED MEASUREMENTS

- Approx 7"/18cm tall and 9"/23cm long

MATERIALS AND TOOLS

- Yarn A (**6** SUPER BULKY): 550 yd/503m of Bulky weight yarn, wool/acrylic/polyester, in light cream
- Yarn B (**4** MEDIUM): 166yd/152m of Worsted weight yarn, merino wool, in black
- Yarn C (**0** LACE): 300yds/174m of Crochet thread, bamboo, in dark brown
- Yarn D (**0** LACE): 300yds/174m of Crochet thread, mercerized cotton, in black
- Size H/8 (5mm) crochet hook OR SIZE TO OBTAIN GAUGE
- Size E/4 (3.5mm) crochet hook OR SIZE TO OBTAIN GAUGE
- Size 7 (1.5mm) steel crochet hook OR SIZE TO OBTAIN GAUGE
- 16oz/500g polyester fiberfill stuffing
- Sewing needle and matching black and cream threads

- Yarn needle
- Scissors

GAUGE

- With Yarn A, 8 sts and 8 rows = 2"/5cm in sc
- With Yarn B, 12 sts and 12 rows = 2"/5cm in sc

TECHNIQUES

- Adjustable ring (page 12)

instructions

Note: The sheep's body and head are firmly stuffed with fiberfill stuffing. To make stuffing easier, begin filling body at round 29 and head at round 27.

BODY AND NECK
(Beg at bum)

Body

Rnd 1 (Adjustable ring): With Yarn A, make a double lp a few inches from end of yarn, leaving a tail in front. With Size H/8 (5mm) crochet hook, draw working yarn through double lp, ch 1, 6 sc into double lp, crocheting over tail, then pull tail to draw lp closed. Join with sl st in 1st sc.

Rnd 2: Ch 1, 2 sc in same sc as joining and in each rem sc. Join with sl st in 1st sc—12 sc.

Rnd 3: Ch 1, sc in same sc as joining, 2 sc in next sc, *sc in next sc, 2 sc in next sc. Rep from * 5 times. Join with sl st in 1st sc—18 sc.

Rnd 4: Ch 1, sc in same sc as joining and in next sc, 2 sc in next sc, *sc in each of next 2 sc, 2 sc in next sc. Rep from * 5 times. Join with sl st in 1st sc—24 sc.

Rnd 5: Ch 1, sc in same sc as joining and in each of next 2 sc, 2 sc in next sc, *sc in each of next 3 sc, 2 sc in next sc. Rep from * 5 times. Join with sl st in 1st sc—30 sc.

Rnd 6: Ch 1, sc in same sc as joining and in each of next 3 sc, 2 sc in next sc, *sc in each of next 4 sc, 2 sc in next sc. Rep from * 5 times. Join with sl st in 1st sc—36 sc.

Rnd 7: Ch 1, sc in same sc as joining and in each of next 4 sc, 2 sc in next sc, *sc in each of next 5 sc, 2 sc in next sc. Rep from * 5 times. Join with sl st in 1st sc—42 sc.

Rnd 8: Ch 1, sc in same sc as joining and in each of next 5 sc, 2 sc in next sc, *sc in each of next 6 sc, 2 sc in next sc. Rep from * 5 times. Join with sl st in 1st sc—48 sc.

Rnd 9: Ch 1, sc in same sc as joining and in each rem sc. Join with sl st in 1st sc.

Rnd 10: Ch 1, sc in same sc as joining and in each of next

6 sc, 2 sc in next sc, *sc in each of next 7 sc, 2 sc in next sc. Rep from * 5 times. Join with sl st in 1st sc—54 sc.

Rnd 11: Rep rnd 9.

Rnd 12: Ch 1, sc in same sc as joining and in each of next 7 sc, 2 sc in next sc, *sc in each of next 8 sc, 2 sc in next sc. Rep from * 5 times. Join with sl st in 1st sc—60 sc.

Rnds 13–21: Rep rnd 9.

Rnd 22: Ch 1, sc in same sc as joining and in each of next 7 sc, sc2tog, *sc in each of next 8 sc, sc2tog. Rep from * 5 times. Join with sl st in 1st sc—54 sc.

Rnd 23: Rep rnd 9.

Rnd 24: Ch 1, sc in same sc as joining and in each of next 6 sc, sc2tog, *sc in each of next 7 sc, sc2tog. Rep from * 5 times. Join with sl st in 1st sc—48 sc.

Rnd 25: Rep rnd 9.

Rnd 26: Ch 1, sc in same sc as joining and in each of next 5 sc, sc2tog, *sc in each of next 6 sc, sc2tog. Rep from * 5 times. Join with sl st in 1st sc—42 sc.

Rnd 27: Ch 1, sc in same sc as joining and in each of next 4 sc, sc2tog, *sc in each of next 5 sc, sc2tog. Rep from * 5 times. Join with sl st in 1st sc—36 sc.

Rnd 28: Ch 1, sc in same sc as joining and in each of next 3 sc, sc2tog, *sc in each of next 4 sc, sc2tog. Rep from * 5 times. Join with sl st in 1st sc—30 sc.

Rnd 29: Ch 1, sc in same sc as joining and in each of next 2 sc, sc2tog, *sc in each of next 3 sc, sc2tog. Rep from * 5 times. Join with sl st in 1st sc—24 sc. Beg filling.

Rnd 30: Ch 1, sc in same sc as joining and in next sc, sc2tog, *sc in each of next 2 sc, sc2tog. Rep from * 5 times. Join with sl st in 1st sc—18 sc.

Rnd 31: Ch 1, sc in same sc as joining, sc2tog, *sc in next sc, sc2tog. Rep from * 5 times. Join with sl st in 1st sc—12 sc. Cut yarn.

Neck

Rnds 32–35: Join Yarn B and working with Size E/4 (3.5mm) crochet hook, rep rnd 9. Fasten off.

Cont to fill, leaving neck edge open.

HEAD
(Beg at mouth)

Working with Size E/4 (3.5mm) crochet hook and Yarn B:

Rnds 1–7: Rep rnds 1–7 of body.

Rnd 8: Rep rnd 9 of body.

Rnd 9: Rep rnd 8 of body—48 sc.

Rnds 10–12: Rep rnd 9 of body.

Rnd 13: Ch 1, sc in same sc as joining and in each of next 13 sc, sc2tog, *sc in each of next 14 sc, sc2tog. Rep from * 3 times. Join with sl st in 1st sc—45 sc.

Rnd 14: Rep rnd 9 of body.

Rnd 15: Ch 1, sc in same sc as joining and in each of next 12 sc, sc2tog, *sc in each of next 13 sc, sc2tog. Rep from * 3 times. Join with sl st in 1st sc—42 sc.

Rnd 16: Rep rnd 9 of body.

Rnd 17: Ch 1, sc in same sc as joining and in each of next 11 sc, sc2tog, *sc in each of next 12 sc, sc2tog. Rep from * 3 times. Join with sl st in 1st sc—39 sc.

Rnd 18: Rep rnd 9 of body.

Rnd 19: Ch 1, sc in same sc as joining and in each of next 10 sc, sc2tog, *sc in each of next 11 sc, sc2tog. Rep from * 3 times. Join with sl st in 1st sc—36 sc.

Rnd 20: Rep rnd 9 of body.

Rnd 21: Ch 1, sc in same sc as joining and in each of next 9 sc, sc2tog, *sc in each of next 10 sc, sc2tog. Rep from * 3 times. Join with sl st in 1st sc—33 sc.

Rnd 22: Rep rnd 9 of body.

Rnd 23: Ch 1, sc in same sc as joining and in each of next 8 sc, sc2tog, *sc in each of next 9 sc, sc2tog. Rep from * 3 times. Join with sl st in 1st sc—30 sc.

Rnds 24–26: Rep rnd 9 of body.

Rnd 27: Rep rnd 29 of body—24 sc. Beg filling.

Rnd 28: Rep rnd 9 of body.

Rnds 29–30: Rep rnds 30–31 of body—12 sc on Rnd 30.

Rnd 31: Ch 1, *sc2tog. Rep from * 6 times. Join with sl st in 1st sc—6 sc. Cut yarn, leaving a 10"/25cm tail. Fill firmly. Insert thread into needle, and run thread through last rnd sts. Draw up tightly and fasten off.

WOOLY CAP
(Beg at top)

Working with Size H/8 (5mm) crochet hook and Yarn A:

Rnds 1–4: Rep rnds 1–4 of body.

Rnds 5–6: Rep rnd 9 of body.

Rnd 7: Join Yarn B, and working with Size E/4 (3.5mm) crochet hook, rep rnd 9 of body. Fasten off.

EARS
(Make 2, beg at bottom)

Working with Size E/4 (3.5mm) crochet hook and Yarn B:

Rnds 1–3: Rep rnds 1–3 of body—18 sc on Rnd 3.

Rnds 4–6: Rep rnd 9 of body.

Rnd 7: Ch 1, sc in same sc as joining and in each of next 3 sc, sc2tog, *sc in each of next 4 sc, sc2tog. Rep from * 3 times. Join with sl st in 1st sc—15 sc.

Rnd 8: Rep rnd 9 of body.

Rnd 9: Ch 1, sc in same sc as joining and in each of next 2 sc, sc2tog, *sc in each of next 3 sc, sc2tog. Rep from * 3 times. Join with sl st in 1st sc—12 sc.

Rnd 10: Rep rnd 9 of body.

Rnd 11: Ch 1, sc in same sc as joining and in next sc, sc2tog, *sc in each of next 2 sc, sc2tog. Rep from * 3 times. Join with sl st in 1st sc—9 sc.

Rnds 12–16: Rep rnd 9 of body. Fasten off.

EYES
(Make 2, beg at pupil)

Working with Size H/7 (1.5mm) crochet hook and Yarn D:

Rnd 1: Rep rnd 1 of body. Cut yarn.

Rnd 2: Join Yarn C and rep rnd 2 of body—12 sc.

Rnds 3–4: Rep rnd 9 of body.

Rnd 5: Ch 1, *sc2tog. Rep from * 6 times. Join with sl st in 1st sc—6 sc. Cut yarn, leaving a 10"/25.5cm tail. Fill firmly. Insert thread into needle, and run thread through last rnd sts. Draw up tightly. Don't cut tail.

LEGS
(Make 4, beg at foot)

Row 1 (Adjustable ring): With Yarn B, make a lp by putting yarn tail behind working yarn. With Size E/4 (3.5mm) crochet hook, draw working yarn through lp, ch 1, 10 sc into lp, crocheting over tail, then pull tail to draw lp closed.

Rnds 2–9: Ch 1, sc in same sc as joining and in each rem sc. Join with sl st in 1st sc—10 sc. Fasten off. Fill firmly, leaving leg edge open.

TAIL
(Beg at bottom)

Working with Size H/8 (5mm) crochet hook and Yarn A:

Rnds 1–3: Rep rnds 1–3 of body—18 sc on rnd 3.

Rnds 4–5: Rep rnd 9 of body.

Rnd 6: Rep rnd 7 of ears—15 sc.

Rnd 7: Rep rnd 9 of ears—12 sc.

Rnd 8: Rep rnd 11 of ears—9 sc.

Rnds 9–11: Rep rnd 9 of body. Fasten off.

ATTACHING PARTS

Attaching wooly cap to head

Place wooly cap on head with bottom of wooly cap corresponding to rnd 23 of head. With black thread, sew wooly cap onto head with whip stitch.

Attaching ears to head

Position ears on either side of head, immediately below wooly cap, and sew on with black thread and whip stitch.

Attaching eyes to head

Position eyes on front of head, 2 rnds below wooly cap. Use uncut tails to sew on.

Attaching head to neck

Position back center of head, 1 rnd below wooly cap, onto neck. Sew on with black thread and whip stitch.

Attaching tail to body

Position tail at upper middle of rnd 10 of body. Sew on with cream thread and whip stitch.

Attaching legs to body

Position hind legs at lower middle of rnd 7 of body, 1"/2.5cm apart. Sew on with cream thread and whip stitch.

Position front legs at lower middle side of rnd 12 of body, 1½"/4cm apart. Sew on with cream thread and whip stitch.

this project was crocheted with

((A) 1 ball of Lion Woolspun Yarn, Bulky weight, 86% wool/9.9% acrylic/4.1% polyester, approx 16oz/454g = 550 yd/503m, color 490-099

(B) 1 ball of Moda Dea Washable Wool, Worsted weight, 100% merino wool, approx 3.5oz/100g =166yd/152m, color 4412

(C) 1 ball of Aunt Lydia's Bamboo Crochet Thread, 100% bamboo, approx 2oz/59g = 300yds/174m, color 0365

(D) 1 ball of Aunt Lydia's South Maid Crochet Thread, 100% mercerized cotton, approx 2oz/59g = 300yds/174m, color 12.

forest floor slippers

For many, slipping on a pair of slippers after a day of work means it's finally time to relax. These forest-colored slippers are as soft as padded moss. Kept by the bedside or beside the front door, they are a welcoming element in home décor.

EXPERIENCE LEVEL

 Intermediate

SIZES

- Woman's 7–9 (10–11)

FINISHED MEASUREMENTS

- 4"/10cm (4½"/11.5cm) along leg

MATERIALS AND TOOLS

- Yarn A **6** SUPER BULKY: 153yds/140m of Bulky weight yarn, acrylic/wool, in dusty green
- Yarn B **6** SUPER BULKY: 153yds/140m of Bulky weight yarn, acrylic/wool, in dark green
- Yarn C **2** FINE: 11yd/10m of thin, 3-strand hemp yarn, in natural beige
- Rope: 150"/381cm of Multi-ply jute twine, approx ³/₁₆"/5mm diameter, in natural beige
- Beige leather square 9"/23cm x 11"/28cm
- Two brown leather laces, 25"/63.5cm long
- Size E/4 (3.5mm) crochet hook OR SIZE TO OBTAIN GAUGE
- Tracing paper, pencil, and permanent marker
- Scissors
- Leather hole punch, 3mm hole

GAUGE

- With Yarn A, 8 sts and 10 rows = 2"/5cm in sc

TECHNIQUES

- Attaching rope to leather piece (page 18)
- Single crochet over rope (page 16)

instructions

SOLE

Copy appropriate sole template onto tracing paper. Mark 3mm holes all around the template edge, ¼"/0.6cm from edge and ²⁄₇"/0.7cm from each other. When spacing holes, measure space between each hole from middle of holes. Cut out, transfer to leather square, trace around template with permanent marker, and cut out leather sole. Punch 3mm holes as marked—about 84 (92) holes.

ATTACHING ROPE TO LEATHER SOLE

Note: If you have exactly 84 (92) holes, follow instructions below for Rnd 1. If you have more holes, make sc instead of 2 sc in some holes. If you have fewer holes, make 2 sc instead of sc in some holes. It is important to finish with 104 (112) sc.

Orient leather with smooth side downwards and heel away from you. Position rope on inner sole with free end to your right and behind holes.

Rnd 1: Curving rope around and above sole, with Yarn C, insert hook in top hole at middle back of sole (heel) and ch 1 over rope, sc over rope in each of next holes around sole. Make 2 sc over rope in holes along sole curve to prevent sole from crumpling. Join with sl st in 1st sc—104 (112) sc.

Rnd 2: Curving rope around and above prev row, ch 1 over rope, sc over rope in same sc as joining and in each of next rem sc. Join with sl st in 1st sc—104 (112) sc. Cut yarn and rope.

BASE

Rnds 3–8 (10): Join Yarn A, ch 1, sc into 1st sc from hook and in each of next rem sc. Join with sl st in 1st sc—104 (112) sc. Fasten off.

UPPER

With toe close to you and sole down, find middle front of slipper and count 10 (12) sts on either side for a total of 20 (24) sts.

Row 1: With Yarn B, insert hook in back lp of rightmost middle sc, ch 1, sc in same sc, inserting hook in back lp only, sc in each of next 19 (23) sc—20 (24) sc.

Rows 2–5 (2–7): Ch 1, inserting hook in back lp only, sc into 1st sc from hook and in each of next rem sc—20 (24) sc.

Row 6 (8) (right slipper): Ch 1, sc into 1st sc from hook and in each of next 17 (21) sc, sk next sc, sc in last sc—19 (23) sc.

Row 6 (8) (left slipper): Ch 1, sc into 1st sc from hook, sk next sc, sc in each of next rem sc—19 (23) sc.

Rows 7–9 (9–11): Ch 1, sc into 1st sc from hook and in each of next rem sc.

Row 10 (12): Rep row 6 (8) for right (left) slipper—18 (22) sc.

Rows 11–13 (13–15): Rep rows 7–9 (9–11).

Row 14 (16): Rep row 6 (8)—17 (21) sc.

Rows 15–17 (17–19): Rep rows 7–9 (9–11).

Row 18 (20): Rep row 6 (8)—16 (20) sc.

Rows 19–21 (21–23): Rep rows 7–9 (9–11). Don't cut yarn.

TONGUE

Row 1: Rep row 6 (8) of upper—15 (19) sc.

Rows 2–4: Rep rows 7–9 (9–11) of upper.

Row 5: Rep row 6 (8) of upper—14 (18) sc.

Rows 6–8: Rep rows 7–9 (9–11) of upper.

Row 9: Rep row 6 (8) of upper—13 (17) sc.

Row 10: Ch 1, sc into 1st sc from hook and in each of next rem sc.

Row 11 (13) (right slipper): Ch 1, sc into 1st sc from hook, 2 sc in next sc, sc in each of next rem sc—14 (18) sc.

Row 11 (13) (left slipper): Ch 1, sc into 1st sc from hook and in each of next 10 sc, 2 sc in next sc, sc in last sc—14 (18) sc.

Row 12: Rep row 10 (10).

Row 13: Rep row 11 (13) for right (left) slipper—15 (19) sc.

Row 14: Rep row 10 (10).

Row 15: Rep row 11 (13)—16 (20) sc.

Row 16: Rep row 10 (10). Fasten off.

ATTACHING UPPER TO BASE

With toe to your left, sole down, and Yarn A, place upper onto base, and insert hook in upper's 20th (22nd) row edge st and in its corresponding st at last row of base [20th (22nd) st from beg of upper]. Ch 1, sc in same pair of sts and in each of next 18 (22) sts along edge of upper and its corresponding sts along last row of base, 2 sc in last pair of sts; 2 sc in unused lp of rightmost middle sc at last row of base (beg of upper) and in each of next 18 (22) unused lps along toe, 2 sc in last unused lp; 2 sc in upper's 1st row edge st and in its corresponding st at last row of base (1st st from beg of upper), sc in each of next 19 (23) sts along edge of upper and its corresponding sts along last row of base. Fasten off.

LEG

Row 1: With toe close to you, sole down, and Yarn A, insert hook in 8th (10th) st at 20th (22nd) row of upper and work 7 (9) overlay chs in each of next 7 (9) sc along 20th (22nd) row of upper; sc in next sc at last row of base and in each of next 43 sc along last row of base (around leg); insert hook in 1st st at 20th (22nd) row of upper and work 7 (9) overlay chs in each of next 7 (9) sc along 20th (22nd) row of upper. Cut yarn.

Row 2: With toe close to you, sole down, and Yarn A, insert hook in back lp of 1st overlay ch at prev row, ch 1, inserting hook in back lp only, sc in same st and in each of next 6 (8) overlay chs. Sk next sc, sc in each of next 42 sc, sk last sc; inserting hook in back lp only, sc in each of next 7 (9) overlay chs.

Row 3: Ch 1, sc into 1st sc from hook, ch 1, sk next sc (for eyelet), sc in each of next 5 (7) sc; sk next sc, sc in each of next 40 sc, sk last sc; sc in each of next 5 (7) sc, ch 1, sk next sc, sc in last sc.

Row 4: Ch 1, sc into 1st sc from hook, sc in ch-1 space, sc in each of next 5 (7) sc; sk next sc, sc in each of next 38 sc, sk last sc; sc in each of next 5 (7) sc, sc in ch-1 space, sc in last sc.

Row 5: Ch 1, sc into 1st sc from hook and in each of next 6 (8) sc; sk next sc, sc in each of next 36 sc, sk last sc; sc in each of next 7 (9) sc.

Rows 6: Ch 1, sc into 1st sc from hook, ch 1, sk next sc (for eyelet), sc in each of next 5 (7) sc; sk next sc, sc in each of next 34 sc, sk last sc; sc in each of next 5 (7) sc, ch 1, sk next sc, sc in last sc.

Row 7: Ch 1, sc into 1st sc from hook, sc in ch-1 space, sc in each of next 5 (7) sc; sk next sc, sc in each of next 32 sc, sk last sc; sc in each of next 5 (7) sc, sc in ch-1 space, sc in last sc.

Row 8: Ch 1, sc into 1st sc from hook and in each of next 6 (8) sc; sk next sc, sc in each of next 30 sc, sk last sc; sc in each of next 7 (9) sc.

Row 9: Ch 1, sc into 1st sc from hook, ch 1, sk next sc (for eyelet), sc in each of next 5 (7) sc; sk next sc, sc in each of next 28 sc, sk last sc; sc in each of next 5 (7) sc, ch 1, sk next sc, sc in last sc.

Row 10: Ch 1, sc into 1st sc from hook, sc in ch-1 space, sc in each of next 5 (7) sc; sk next sc, sc in each of next 26 sc, sk last sc; sc in each of next 5 (7) sc, sc in ch-1 space, sc in last sc.

Row 11: Ch 1, sc into 1st sc from hook and in each of next 6 (8) sc; sk next sc, sc in each of next 24 sc, sk last sc; sc in each of next 7 (9) sc.

Row 12: Ch 1, sc into 1st sc from hook and in each of next rem sc 38 (42) sc. Fasten off.

CROCHETING EDGES

Crocheting around eyelet tab and leg opening

With toe to your right, sole down, and Yarn A, insert hook in 1st row edge st of leg (bottom of eyelet tab), ch 1, sc in same st and in each of next 10 edge sts along eyelet tab, from bottom to top, 2 sc in last st and in next sc around leg opening, sc in each of next 36 (40) sc around leg opening, 2 sc in last sc and in next edge st along eyelet tab, sc in each of next 11 edge sts along eyelet tab from top to bottom. Fasten off.

Crocheting around visible part of tongue

Fasten tongue in place by sewing its 6th row from top edge st to corresponding place on eyelet tab.

With toe to your right, sole down, and Yarn A, insert hook in 5th row from top edge st of tongue, ch 1, sc in same st and in each of next 3 edge sts along tongue edge, from bottom to top, 2 sc in last st and in next sc at last row of tongue, sc in each of next 14 (18) sc at last row of tongue, 2 sc in last sc and in next edge st along tongue edge, sc in each of next 4 edge sts along tongue edge from top to bottom. Fasten off.

Insert leather lace.

this project was crocheted with

(A) 1 ball of Lion Wool-Ease Chunky Yarn, 80% acrylic/20% wool, bulky weight, approx 5oz/140g = 153yrds/140m per ball, color 630-173

(B) 1 ball of Lion Wool-Ease Chunky Yarn, 80% acrylic/20% wool, bulky weight, approx 5oz/140g = 153yrds/140m per ball, color 630-180

(C) 1 spool of HempBasics, 100% hemp 3-strand yarn, approx 17.6oz/500g = 1800yd/ 1642m per spool

(Rope) 3-ply jute twine, 100% jute, approx 3/16"/5mm diameter, in natural beige

rounds-in-a-rectangle runner

This runner features an unusual design that perfectly suits supporting several dishes, coffee cups, or small vases. It can be folded up and stored as a small tower, then spread out with ease onto a table or dresser top.

EXPERIENCE LEVEL

◼◼◻◻ Easy

FINISHED MEASUREMENTS

- 29"/73.5cm x 16"/40.5cm)

MATERIALS AND TOOLS

- Yarn A (4 MEDIUM): 145yd/132m of Medium weight yarn, recycled cotton/acrylic, in orange
- Yarn B (4 MEDIUM): 145yd/132m of Medium weight yarn, recycled cotton/acrylic, in dusty green
- Yarn C (4 MEDIUM): 145yd/132m of Medium weight yarn, recycled cotton/acrylic, in dusty blue
- Rope: 150"/381cm of Multi-ply jute twine, approx ³⁄₁₆"/5mm diameter, in natural beige
- Beige leather square 9"/23cm x 11"/28cm
- Two brown leather laces, 25"/63.5cm long
- Size E/4 (3.5mm) crochet hook OR SIZE TO OBTAIN GAUGE
- Tracing paper, pencil, and permanent marker
- Scissors
- Leather hole punch, 3mm hole

GAUGE

- With Yarn A, 11 sts and 9 rows = 2"/5cm in sc

SPECIAL STITCHES

- Overlay chain stitch (page 9)

TECHNIQUES

- Attaching to frame (page 13)

instructions

ROUND PLACEMAT 1

Foundation row: With Yarn A, ch 5, join with sl st in 1st ch to form a ring.

Rnd 1: Ch 1, 8 sc in ring. Join with sl st in 1st sc.

Rnd 2: Ch 1, inserting hook in back lp only, 2 sc in same sc as joining and in each rem sc. Join with sl st in 1st sc—16 sc.

Rnd 3: Ch 1, inserting hook in back lp only, sc in same sc as joining, 2 sc in next sc, *sc in next sc, 2 sc in next sc. Rep from * 7 times. Join with sl st in 1st sc—24 sc.

Rnd 4: Ch 1, inserting hook in back lp only, sc in same sc as joining and in next sc, 2 sc in next sc, *sc in each of next 2 sc, 2 sc in next sc. Rep from * 7 times. Join with sl st in 1st sc—32 sc.

Rnd 5: Ch 1, inserting hook in back lp only, sc in same sc as joining and in each of next 2 sc, 2 sc in next sc, *sc in each of next 3 sc, 2 sc in next sc. Rep from * 7 times. Join with sl st in 1st sc—40 sc.

Rnd 6: Ch 1, inserting hook in back lp only, sc in same sc as joining and in each of next 3 sc, 2 sc in next sc, *sc in each of next 4 sc, 2 sc in next sc. Rep from * 7 times. Join with sl st in 1st sc—48 sc.

Rnd 7: Ch 1, inserting hook in back lp only, sc in same sc as joining and in each of next 4 sc, 2 sc in next sc, *sc in each of next 5 sc, 2 sc in next sc. Rep from * 7 times. Join with sl st in 1st sc—56 sc.

Rnd 8: Ch 1, inserting hook in back lp only, sc in same sc as joining and in each of next 5 sc, 2 sc in next sc, *sc in each of next 6 sc, 2 sc in next sc. Rep from * 7 times. Join with sl st in 1st sc—64 sc.

Rnd 9: Ch 1, inserting hook in back lp only, sc in same sc as joining and in each of next 6 sc, 2 sc in next sc, *sc in each of next 7 sc, 2 sc in next sc. Rep from * 7 times. Join with sl st in 1st sc—72 sc. Cut yarn.

Rnd 10: Join Yarn B, ch 1, inserting hook in back lp only, sc in same sc as joining and in each of next 7 sc, 2 sc in next sc, *sc in each of next 8 sc, 2 sc in next sc. Rep from * 7 times. Join with sl st in 1st sc—80 sc.

Rnd 11: Ch 1, inserting hook in back lp only, sc in same sc as joining and in each of next 8 sc, 2 sc in next sc, *sc in each of next 9 sc, 2 sc in next sc. Rep from * 7 times. Join with sl st in 1st sc—88 sc.

Rnd 12: Ch 1, inserting hook in back lp only, sc in same sc as joining and in each of next 9 sc, 2 sc in next sc, *sc in each of next 10 sc, 2 sc in next sc. Rep from * 7 times. Join with sl st in 1st sc—96 sc.

Rnd 13: Ch 1, inserting hook in back lp only, sc in same sc as joining and in each of next 10 sc, 2 sc in next sc, *sc in each of next 11 sc, 2 sc in next sc. Rep from * 7 times. Join with sl st in 1st sc—104 sc.

Rnd 14: Ch 1, inserting hook in back lp only, sc in same sc as joining and in each of next 11 sc, 2 sc in next sc, *sc in each of next 12 sc, 2 sc in next sc. Rep from * 7 times. Join with sl st in 1st sc—112 sc. Fasten off.

ROUND PLACEMAT 2

Foundation row: Rep foundation row of round placemat 1.

Rnds 1–8: Rep rnds 1–8 of round placemat 1. Cut yarn.

Rnds 9–14: Join Yarn B and rep rnds 9–14 of round placemat 1. Fasten off.

ROUND PLACEMAT 3

Foundation row: Rep foundation row of round placemat 1.

Rnds 1–8: Rep rnds 1–8 of round placemat 1. Cut yarn.

Rnds 9–12: Join Yarn B and rep rnds 9–12 of round placemat 1. Fasten off.

ROUND PLACEMAT 4

Foundation row: Rep foundation row of round placemat 1.

Rnds 1–7: Rep rnds 1–7 of round placemat 1. Cut yarn.

Rnds 8–12: Join Yarn B and rep rnds 8–12 of round placemat 1. Fasten off.

ROUND PLACEMAT 5

Foundation row: Rep foundation row of round placemat 1.

Rnds 1–7: Rep rnds1–7 of round placemat 1. Cut yarn.

Rnds 8–10: Join Yarn B and rep rnds 8–10 of round placemat 1. Fasten off.

ROUND PLACEMAT 6

Foundation row: Rep foundation row of round placemat 1.

Rnds 1–6: Rep rnds 1–6 of round placemat 1. Cut yarn.

Rnds 7–10: Join Yarn B and rep rnds 7–10 of round placemat 1. Fasten off.

ROUND PLACEMAT 7

Foundation row: Rep foundation row of round placemat 1.

Rnds 1–6: Rep rnds 1–6 of round placemat 1. Cut yarn.

Rnds 7–8: Join Yarn B and rep rnds 7–8 of round placemat 1. Fasten off.

ROUND PLACEMAT 8

Foundation row: Rep foundation row of round placemat 1.

Rnds 1–5: Rep rnds 1–5 of round placemat 1. Cut yarn.

Rnds 6–8: Join Yarn B and rep rnds 6–8 of round placemat 1. Fasten off.

CROCHETED RECTANGLE FRAME

Note: The round placemats in this runner are crocheted separately, then attached to the frame. Marking the connection points A through L on the frame as it is crocheted makes it easier to explain where to attach the pieces later.

With Yarn C, ch 400, join with sl st in 1st ch to form a ring.

Place stitch markers on: 18th ch (*A*); 50th ch (*B*); 86th ch (*C*); 118th ch (*D*); 150th ch (*E*); 182nd ch (*F*); 219th ch (*G*); 251st ch (*H*); 286th ch (*I*); 318th ch (*J*); 350th ch (*K*); 382nd ch (*L*).

Rnd 1: Ch 1, sc in same ch as joining and in each of next 399 chs, placing stitch markers on increase points (corners), while working. Join with sl st in 1st sc—400 sc.

Place stitch markers on: 69th sc, 200th sc, 269th sc, 400th sc.

Rnd 2: Ch 1, inserting hook in back lp only, sc in same sc as joining and in each of next 67 sc, 3 sc in 69th sc, sc in each of next 130 sc, 3 sc in 200th sc, sc in each of next 68 sc, 3 sc in 269th sc, sc in each of next 130 sc, 3 sc in 400th sc, replacing stitch markers on increase points (corners), while working. Join with sl st in 1st sc—408 sc.

Place stitch markers on: 70th sc, 203rd sc, 274th sc, 407th sc.

Rnd 3: Ch 1, inserting hook in back lp only, sc in same sc as joining and in each of next 68 sc, 3 sc in 70th sc, sc in each of next 132 sc, 3 sc in 203rd sc, sc in each of next 70 sc, 3 sc in 274th sc, sc in each of next 132 sc, 3 sc in 407th sc, sc in last sc—416 sc. Fasten off.

ATTACHING PIECES

Note: Inner bottom of crocheted rectangle frame is first 68 sts.

1st long column

With RS of round placemats 8, 6, 4, and 2, and RS of crocheted rectangle frame facing, bottom close to you, and Yarn A, insert hook in A, ch 10.

With lp on hook, insert hook in last rnd, last sc of round placemat 8, and work 16 overlay chs across round placemat 8 diameter, inserting hook in each rnd. Ch 14

With lp on hook, insert hook in last rnd, last sc of round placemat 6, and work 20 overlay chs across round placemat 6 diameter, inserting hook in each rnd. Ch 10.

With lp on hook, insert hook in last rnd, last sc of round placemat 4, and work 24 overlay chs across round placemat 4 diameter, inserting hook in each rnd. Ch 6.

With lp on hook, insert hook in last rnd, last sc of round placemat 2, and work 28 overlay chs across round placemat 2 diameter, inserting hook in each rnd. Ch 4.

With lp on hook, insert hook in H, overlay ch 1. Fasten off.

2nd long column

With RS of round placemats 7, 5, 3, and 1, and RS of crocheted rectangle frame facing, bottom away from you, and Yarn A, insert hook in G, ch 10.

Rep instructions for 1st long column, replacing round placemats 8, 6, 4, 2 with 7, 5, 3, 1, respectively. With lp on hook, insert hook in B, overlay ch 1. Fasten off.

1st short column

With RS of rectangle frame facing and bottom to your right, insert hook in *L*, ch 10.

With lp on hook, insert hook in last rnd, last sc of round placemat 8, and work 16 overlay chs across round placemat 8 diameter, inserting hook in each rnd. Ch 10.

With lp on hook, insert hook in last rnd, last sc of round placemat 1, and work 28 overlay chs across round placemat 1 diameter, inserting hook in each rnd. Ch 4.

With lp on hook, insert hook in *C*, overlay ch 1. Fasten off.

2nd short column

With RS of rectangle frame facing and bottom to your right, insert hook in *K*, ch 8.

With lp on hook, insert hook in last rnd, last sc of round placemat 6, and work 20 overlay chs across round placemat 6 diameter, inserting hook in each rnd. Ch 10.

With lp on hook, insert hook in last rnd, last sc of round placemat 3, and work 24 overlay chs across round placemat 3 diameter, inserting hook in each rnd. Ch 6.

With lp on hook, insert hook in *D*, overlay ch 1. Fasten off.

3rd (4th) short columns

With RS of crocheted rectangle frame facing, bottom to your left, and Yarn A, insert hook in *F* (*E*), ch 10 (8).

Rep instructions for 1st (2nd) short columns, replacing round placemats 8 and 1 (6 and 3) with round placemats 7 and 2 (5 and 4), respectively. With lp on hook, insert hook in *I* (*J*), overlay ch 1. Fasten off.

this project was crocheted with

(A) 1 ball of Red Heart Eco-Cotton Blend, 75% recycled cotton/25% acrylic, medium weight, approx 3oz/85g = 145yd/132m per ball, color 1255

(B) 1 ball of Red Heart Eco-Cotton Blend, 75% recycled cotton/25% acrylic, medium weight, approx 3oz/85g = 145yd/132m per ball, color 1645

(C) 1 ball of Red Heart Eco-Cotton Blend, 75% recycled cotton/25% acrylic, medium weight, approx 3oz/85g = 145yd/132m per ball, color 1870

spiraling placemat

With its round shape and spiral pattern, this placemat mimics the mathematical shapes in nature. The technique involves crocheting over a thick rope, making it particularly sturdy and resistant to heat.

EXPERIENCE LEVEL

■■■■ □ □) Easy

FINISHED MEASUREMENTS

- 13½"/34.5cm diameter

MATERIALS AND TOOLS

- Yarn A **4** (MEDIUM): 249yd/228m of Medium weight yarn, recycled cotton/acrylic, in dusty blue

- Yarn B **4** (MEDIUM): 145yd/132m of Medium weight yarn, recycled cotton/acrylic, in orange

- Rope: 55yd/50m of Multi-ply jute twine, approx ³⁄₁₆"/5mm diameter, in natural beige

- Size E/4 (3.5mm) crochet hook OR SIZE TO OBTAIN GAUGE

- Scissors

- Iron (for blocking)

GAUGE

- With Yarn A, 8 sts and 6 rows= 2"/5cm in sc over rope

TECHNIQUES

- Foundation row over rope (page 14)

- Foundation round over rope (page 15)

- Single crochet over rope (page 16)

instructions

Foundation row: With free end of rope to your right and Yarn B, ch 1 over rope (leaving 1"/2.5cm tail of rope), 12 sc along and over rope.

Rnd 1: Curving foundation row into a ring and carrying rope and yarn above, connect ring by making 2 sc over rope into 1st sc of foundation row. Curving rope around foundation row, 2 sc over rope in next sc. Join Yarn A, 2 sc over rope in each of next 10 sc—24 sc.

Note: Curve rope around each of next rounds, making a round shape, and following instructions below. Block (page 9) while working to prevent shape from crumpling.

Rnd 2: *Sc over rope in next sc, 2 sc over rope in next sc. Rep from * twice. With Yarn B, rep from * 10 times—36 sc.

Rnd 3: *Sc over rope in next 2 sc, 2 sc over rope in next sc. Rep from * twice. With Yarn A, rep from * 10 times—48 sc.

Rnd 4: *Sc over rope in next 3 sc, 2 sc over rope in next sc. Rep from * twice. With Yarn B, holding rope and Yarn A tog, sc over rope and Yarn A in next 3 sc, 2 sc over rope and Yarn A in next sc. With Yarn A, rep from * 9 times—60 sc.

Rnd 5: *Sc over rope in next 4 sc, 2 sc over rope in next sc. Rep from * 3 times. With Yarn B, rep from * 9 times—72 sc. Cut Yarn A.

Rnd 6: *Sc over rope in next 5 sc, 2 sc over rope in next sc. Rep from * twice. Join Yarn A, rep from * 10 times—84 sc.

Rnd 7: *Sc over rope in next 6 sc, 2 sc over rope in next sc. Rep from * twice. With Yarn B, holding rope and Yarn A tog, sc over rope and Yarn A in next 6 sc, 2 sc over rope and Yarn A in next sc. With Yarn A, rep from * 9 times—96 sc.

Rnd 8: *Sc over rope in next 7 sc, 2 sc over rope in next sc. Rep from * 3 times. With Yarn B, holding rope and Yarn A tog, sc over rope and Yarn A in next 7 sc, 2 sc over rope and Yarn A in next sc. With Yarn A, rep from * 8 times—108 sc.

Rnd 9: *Sc over rope in next 8 sc, 2 sc over rope in next sc. Rep from * 4 times. With Yarn B, rep from * 8 times—120 sc. Cut Yarn A.

Rnd 10: *Sc over rope in next 9 sc, 2 sc over rope in next sc. Rep from * twice. Join Yarn A, rep from * 10 times—132 sc.

Rnd 11: *Sc over rope in next 10 sc, 2 sc over rope in next sc. Rep from * twice. With Yarn B, holding rope and Yarn A tog, sc over rope and Yarn A in next 10 sc, 2 sc over rope and Yarn A in next sc. With Yarn A, rep from * 9 times—144 sc.

Rnd 12: *Sc over rope in next 11 sc, 2 sc over rope in next sc. Rep from * 3 times. With Yarn B, holding rope and Yarn A tog, sc over rope and Yarn A in next 11 sc, 2 sc over rope and Yarn A in next sc. With Yarn A, rep from * 8 times—156 sc.

Rnd 13: *Sc over rope in next 12 sc, 2 sc over rope in next sc. Rep from * 4 times. With Yarn B, holding rope and Yarn A tog, sc over rope and Yarn A in next 12 sc, 2 sc over rope and Yarn A in next sc. With Yarn A, rep from * 7 times—168 sc.

Rnd 14: *Sc over rope in next 13 sc, 2 sc over rope in next sc. Rep from * 5 times. With Yarn B, rep from * 7 times—180 sc. Cut Yarn A.

Rnd 15: *Sc over rope in next 14 sc, 2 sc over rope in next sc. Rep from * twice. Join Yarn A, rep from * 10 times—192 sc.

Rnd 16: *Sc over rope in next 15 sc, 2 sc over rope in next sc. Rep from * twice. With Yarn B, holding rope and Yarn A tog, sc over rope and Yarn A in next 15 sc, 2 sc over rope and Yarn A in next sc. With Yarn A, rep from * 9 times—204 sc.

Rnd 17: *Sc over rope in next 16 sc, 2 sc over rope in next sc. Rep from * 3 times. With Yarn B, holding rope and Yarn A tog, sc over rope and Yarn A in next 16 sc, 2 sc over rope and Yarn A in next sc. With Yarn A, rep from * 8 times—216 sc.

Rnd 18: *Sc over rope in next 17 sc, 2 sc over rope in next sc. Rep from * 4 times. With Yarn B, holding rope and Yarn A tog, sc over rope and Yarn A in next 17 sc, 2 sc over rope and Yarn A in next sc. With Yarn A, rep from * 7 times—228 sc.

Rnd 19: *Sc over rope in next 18 sc, 2 sc over rope in next sc. Rep from * 5 times. With Yarn B, holding rope and Yarn A tog, sc over rope and Yarn A in next 18 sc, 2 sc over rope and Yarn A in next sc. With Yarn A, rep from * 6 times—240 sc. Cut Yarn B.

Rnd 20 (incomplete rnd): *Sc over rope in next 19 sc, 2 sc over rope in next sc. Rep from * 6 times. Cut rope, leaving a 6"/15cm tail for eyelet. Don't cut yarn.

EYELET

Fold tail in half, with free end on top. Sc over folded rope in next 3 sc. Fasten off.

this project was crocheted with

(A) 2 balls of Red Heart Eco-Cotton Blend, 75% recycled cotton/25% acrylic, medium weight, approx 3oz/85g = 145yd/132m per ball, color 1870

(B) 1 ball of Red Heart Eco-Cotton Blend, 75% recycled cotton/25% acrylic, medium weight, approx 3oz/85g = 145yd/132m per ball, color 1255

(Rope) 3-ply jute twine, 100% jute, approx ³⁄₁₆"/5mm diameter, in natural beige

flat earth placemat

Using blue and green colors to evoke the earth, this placemat is a study in contrast and harmony, and a perfect match for the Spiraling Placement (page 81). This placement also features a handy eyelet, for hanging the placement when it's not in use.

EXPERIENCE LEVEL

■◼◻◻ Easy

FINISHED MEASUREMENTS

- 13"/33cm x 13"/33cm

MATERIALS AND TOOLS

- Yarn A **MEDIUM 4**: 290yd/264m of Medium weight yarn, recycled cotton/acrylic, in dusty blue
- Yarn B **MEDIUM 4**: 145yd/132m of Medium weight yarn, recycled cotton/acrylic, in dusty green
- Rope: 55yd/50m of Multi-ply jute twine, approx 3/16"/5mm diameter, in natural beige
- Size E/4 (3.5mm) crochet hook OR SIZE TO OBTAIN GAUGE
- Scissors

GAUGE

- With Yarn A, 8 sts and 6 rows= 2"/5cm in sc over rope

TECHNIQUES

- Foundation row over rope (page 14)
- Foundation round over rope (page 15)
- Single crochet over rope (page 16)

instructions

Foundation row: With free end of rope to your right and Yarn B, ch 1 over rope (leaving 1"/2.5cm tail of rope), 12 sc along and over rope.

Rnd 1: Curving foundation row into a ring, and carrying rope and yarn above, connect ring by making 2 sc over rope into 1st sc of foundation row. Curving rope around foundation row, 2 sc over rope in next sc. Join Yarn A, 2 sc over rope in each of next 10 sc—24 sc.

Note: Curve rope around each of next rounds, making a square shape, and following instructions below. Block (page 9) while working to prevent shape from crumpling.

Rnd 2: *2 sc over rope in each of next 3 sc, sc over rope in each of next 3 sc.

Rep from * 4 times—36 sc.

Rnd 3: Sc over rope in each of next 2 sc, 2 sc over rope in each of next 2 sc.

*Sc over rope in each of next 7 sc, 2 sc over rope in each of next 2 sc. Rep from * 3 times. Sc over rope in each of next 5 sc—44 sc.

Rnd 4: With Yarn A, sc over rope in each of next 3 sc, 2 sc over rope in each of next 2 sc. *Sc over rope in each of next 9 sc, 2 sc over rope in each of next 2 sc. Rep from * 3 times. Sc over rope in each of next 6 sc—52 sc.

Rnd 5: With Yarn B, sc over rope in each of next 4 sc, 2 sc over rope in each of next 2 sc. *Sc over rope in each of next 11 sc, 2 sc over rope in each of next 2 sc. Rep from * 3 times. Sc over rope in each of next 7 sc—60 sc.

Rnd 6: With Yarn A, sc over rope in each of next 5 sc, 2 sc over rope in each of next 2 sc. *Sc over rope in each of next 13 sc, 2 sc over rope in each of next 2 sc. Rep from * 3 times. Sc over rope in each of next 8 sc—68 sc.

Rnd 7: Sc over rope in each of next 6 sc, 2 sc over rope in each of next 2 sc. *Sc over rope in each of next 15 sc, 2 sc over rope in each of next 2 sc. Rep from * 3 times. Sc over rope in each of next 9 sc—76 sc.

Rnd 8: With Yarn B, sc over rope in each of next 7 sc, 2 sc over rope in each of next 2 sc. *Sc over rope in each of next 17 sc, 2 sc over rope in each of next 2 sc. Rep from * 3 times. Sc over rope in each of next 10 sc—84 sc. Cut yarn.

Rnd 9: With Yarn A, sc over rope in each of next 8 sc, 2 sc over rope in each of next 2 sc. *Sc over rope in each of next 19 sc, 2 sc over rope in each of next 2 sc. Rep from * 3 times. Sc over rope in each of next 11 sc—92 sc.

Rnd 10: Sc over rope in each of next 9 sc, 2 sc over rope in each of next 2 sc. *Sc over rope in each of next 21 sc, 2 sc over rope in each of next 2 sc. Rep from * 3 times. Sc over rope in each of next 12 sc—100 sc.

Rnd 11: Sc over rope in each of next 10 sc, 2 sc over rope in each of next 2 sc. *Sc over rope in each of next 23 sc, 2 sc over rope in each of next 2 sc. Rep from * 3 times. Sc over rope in each of next 13 sc—108 sc.

Rnd 12: Join Yarn B, sc over rope in each of next 11 sc, 2 sc over rope in each of next 2 sc. *Sc over rope in each of next 25 sc, 2 sc over rope in each of next 2 sc. Rep from * 3 times. Sc over rope in each of next 14 sc—116 sc. Cut yarn.

Rnd 13: With Yarn A, sc over rope in each of next 12 sc, 2 sc over rope in each of next 2 sc. *Sc over rope in each of next 27 sc, 2 sc over rope in each of next 2 sc. Rep from * 3 times. Sc over rope in each of next 15 sc—124 sc.

Rnd 14: Sc over rope in each of next 12 sc, 2 sc over rope in each of next 4 sc. *Sc over rope in each of next 27 sc, 2 sc over rope in each of next 4 sc.

Rep from * 3 times. Sc over rope in each of next 15 sc—140 sc.

Rnd 15: Sc over rope in each of next 15 sc, 2 sc over rope in each of next 2 sc. *Sc over rope in each of next 33 sc, 2 sc over rope in each of next 2 sc. Rep from * 3 times. Sc over rope in each of next 18 sc—148 sc.

Rnd 16: Sc over rope in each of next 16 sc, 2 sc over rope in each of next 2 sc. *Sc over rope in each of next 35 sc, 2 sc over rope in each of next 2 sc. Rep from * 3 times. Sc over rope in each of next 19 sc—156 sc.

Rnd 17: Join Yarn B, sc over rope in each of next 16 sc, 2 sc over rope in each of next 4 sc. *Sc over rope in each of next 35 sc, 2 sc over rope in each of next 4 sc. Rep from * 3 times. Sc over rope in each of next 19 sc—172 sc. Cut yarn.

Rnd 18: With Yarn A, sc over rope in each of next 19 sc, 2 sc over rope in each of next 2 sc. *Sc over rope in each of next 41 sc, 2 sc over rope in each of next 2 sc. Rep from * 3 times. Sc over rope in each of next 22 sc—180 sc.

Rnd 19: Sc over rope in each of next 19 sc, 2 sc over rope in each of next 4 sc. *Sc over rope in each of next 41 sc, 2 sc over rope in each of next 4 sc.

Rep from * 3 times. Sc over rope in each of next 22 sc —196 sc.

Rnd 20: Sc over rope in each of next 22 sc, 2 sc over rope in each of next 2 sc. *Sc over rope in each of next 47 sc, 2 sc over rope in each of next 2 sc. Rep from * 3 times. Sc over rope in each of next 25 sc—204 sc.

Rnd 21: Sc over rope in each of next 22 sc, 2 sc over rope in each of next 4 sc. *Sc over rope in each of next 47 sc, 2 sc over rope in each of next 4 sc.

Rep from * 3 times. Sc over rope in each of next 25 sc —220 sc.

Rnd 22: Sc over rope in each of next 25 sc, 2 sc over rope in each of next 2 sc. *Sc over rope in each of next 53 sc, 2 sc over rope in each of next 2 sc. Rep from * 3 times. Sc over rope in each of next 28 sc—228 sc.

Cut rope, leaving a 6"/15cm tail for eyelet. Don't cut yarn.

EYELET

Fold tail in half, with free end on top. Sc over folded rope in next 3 sc. Fasten off.

this project was crocheted with

(A) 2 balls of Red Heart Eco-Cotton Blend, 75% recycled cotton/25% acrylic, medium weight, approx 3oz/85g = 145yd/132m per ball, color 1870

(B) 1 ball of Red Heart Eco-Cotton Blend, 75% recycled cotton/25% acrylic, medium weight, approx 3oz/85g = 145yd/132m per ball, color 1645

(Rope) 3-ply jute twine, 100% jute, approx $^3/_{16}$"/5mm diameter, in natural beige

sunny sunflower apron

This apron isn't just lovely to look at; it's very practical too, since it comes with a slip-on protective cover that protects the apron as you cook.

EXPERIENCE LEVEL

Intermediate

FINISHED MEASUREMENTS

- Apron width: 15"/38cm at top, 18"/45.5cm at bottom

- Apron length: 14"/38cm (without cover)

- Length of waist strap: 67"/170cm

MATERIALS AND TOOLS

- Yarn A (MEDIUM 4): 290yd/264m of Medium weight yarn, recycled cotton/acrylic, in gray

- Yarn B (MEDIUM 4): 145yd/132m of Medium weight yarn, recycled cotton/acrylic, in dark brown

- Yarn C (MEDIUM 4): 207yd/188m of Medium worsted weight yarn, cotton/acrylic, in dark olive green

- Yarn D (MEDIUM 4): 207yd/188m of Medium worsted weight yarn, cotton/acrylic, in dark yellow

- 20"/51cm x 30"/76cm piece of Medium weight clear plastic fabric

- Size E/4 (3.5mm) crochet hook OR SIZE TO OBTAIN GAUGE

- Straight pins

- Stitch marker

- Sewing needle and matching thread

- 15"/38cm x 19"/48.5cm piece of tissue paper

- Pencil

- Scissors

- Leather hole punch, 3mm hole

GAUGE

- With Yarn A, 12 sts and 5 rows = 2"/5cm in dc, ch 1 pattern

SPECIAL STITCHES

- Picot: Ch 3, sl st in 1st ch of ch-3 (page 10)

Protective Plastic Cover

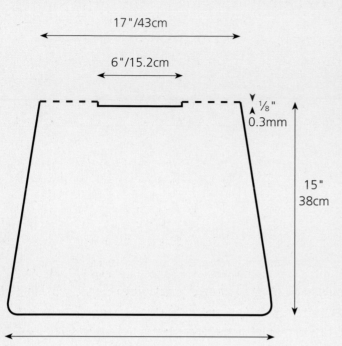

17"/43cm

6"/15.2cm

⅛"
0.3mm

15"
38cm

19"/48.5cm

instructions

WAIST STRAP

With Yarn A, ch 303.

Row 1: Dc in 4th ch from hook and in each of next 300 chs, placing stitch marker on 115th dc (joining point), while working—300 dc. Fasten off.

APRON

Row 1: With RS of waist strap facing, bottom close to you and Yarn A, insert hook in back lp only of 115th dc of waist strap, ch 3, inserting hook in back lp only, dc in each of next 70 dc of waist strap—71 dc.

Row 2: Ch 3, dc in 2nd dc from hook and in each of next 2 dc; *ch 1, sk next dc, dc in next dc. Rep from * 32 times. Dc in each of next 3 dc—32 ch-1 spaces and 39 dc.

Row 3: Ch 3, dc in 2nd dc from hook and in each of next 2 dc; *ch 1, dc in next dc. Rep from * 32 times. Dc in each of next 3 dc—32 ch-1 spaces and 39 dc.

Row 4: Ch 3, dc in 2nd dc from hook, 2 dc in next dc; *ch 1, dc in next dc. Rep from * 33 times. Ch 1, 2 dc in next dc, dc in each of next 2 dc—34 ch-1 spaces and 41 dc.

Rows 5–6: Ch 3, dc in 2nd dc from hook and in each of next 2 dc; *ch 1, dc in next dc. Rep from * 34 times. Dc in each of next 3 dc—34 ch-1 spaces and 41 dc.

Row 7: Ch 3, dc in 2nd dc from hook, 2 dc in next dc; *ch 1, dc in next dc. Rep from * 35 times. Ch1, 2 dc in next dc, dc in each of next 2 dc—36 ch-1 spaces and 43 dc.

Rows 8–9: Ch 3, dc in 2nd dc from hook and in each of next 2 dc; *ch 1, dc in next dc. Rep from * 36 times. Dc in each of next 3 dc—36 ch-1 spaces and 43 dc.

Row 10: Ch 3, dc in 2nd dc from hook, 2 dc in next dc; *ch 1, dc in next dc. Rep from * 37 times. Ch1, 2 dc in next dc, dc in each of next 2 dc—38 ch-1 spaces and 45 dc.

Rows 11–12: Ch 3, dc in 2nd dc from hook and in each of next 2 dc; *ch 1, dc in next dc. Rep from * 38 times. Dc in each of next 3 dc—38 ch-1 spaces and 45 dc.

Row 13: Ch 3, dc in 2nd dc from hook, 2 dc in next dc; *ch 1, dc in next dc. Rep from * 39 times. Ch1, 2 dc in next dc, dc in each of next 2 dc—40 ch-1 spaces and 47 dc.

Rows 14–15: Ch 3, dc in 2nd dc from hook and in each of next 2 dc; *ch 1, dc in next dc. Rep from * 40 times. Dc in each of next 3 dc—40 ch-1 spaces and 47 dc.

Row 16: Ch 3, dc in 2nd dc from hook, 2 dc in next dc; *ch 1, dc in next dc. Rep from * 41 times. Ch1, 2 dc in next dc, dc in each of next 2 dc—42 ch-1 spaces and 49 dc.

Rows 17–18: Ch 3, dc in 2nd dc from hook and in each of next 2 dc; *ch 1, dc in next dc. Rep from * 42 times. Dc in each of next 3 dc—42 ch-1 spaces and 49 dc.

Row 19: Ch 3, dc in 2nd dc from hook, 2 dc in next dc; *ch 1, dc in next dc. Rep from * 43 times. Ch1, 2 dc in next dc, dc in each of next 2 dc—44 ch-1 spaces and 51 dc.

Rows 20–21: Ch 3, dc in 2nd dc from hook and in each of next 2 dc; *ch 1, dc in next dc. Rep from * 44 times. Dc in each of next 3 dc—44 ch-1 spaces and 51 dc.

Row 22: Ch 3, dc in 2nd dc from hook, 2 dc in next dc; *ch 1, dc in next dc. Rep from * 45 times. Ch1, 2 dc in next dc, dc in each of next 2 dc—46 ch-1 spaces and 53 dc.

Rows 23–24: Ch 3, dc in 2nd dc from hook and in each of next 2 dc; *ch 1, dc in next dc. Rep from * 46 times. Dc in each of next 3 dc—46 ch-1 spaces and 53 dc.

Row 25: Ch 3, dc in 2nd dc from hook, 2 dc in next dc; *ch 1, dc in next dc. Rep from * 47 times. Ch1, 2 dc in next dc, dc in each of next 2 dc—48 ch-1 spaces and 55 dc.

Rows 26–29: Ch 3, dc in 2nd dc from hook and in each of next 2 dc; *ch 1, dc in next dc. Rep from * 48 times. Dc in each of next 3 dc—48 ch-1 spaces and 55 dc.

Row 30: Ch 3, dc in 2nd dc from hook and in each of next 2 dc; *ch 1, dc in each of next 2 dc. Rep from * 11 times. Dc in each of next 3 dc; **dc in each of next 2 dc, ch 1. Rep from ** 11 times. Dc in each of next 4 dc—22 ch-1 spaces and 55 dc.

Row 31–32: Ch 3, dc in 2nd dc from hook and in each of next 53 dc—55 dc. Fasten off.

CROCHETING WAIST STRAP EDGES

With RS facing, waist strap away from you, and Yarn B, insert hook in rightmost ch of foundation chs of waist strap, *picot, sk next ch of foundation chs, sl st in next ch of foundation chs. Rep from * 150 times. Cont to work around waist strap and picot, sl st in next ch-3 space, sl st in 1st dc; **picot, sk next dc, sl st in next dc. Rep from ** 57 times. Cont to work along joined edge of waist strap and ***picot, sk next unused lp of dc, sl st in next unused lp. Rep from *** 35 times and from ** 57 times. Picot, sl st in next dc space. Join with sl st in rightmost ch of foundation chs of waist strap. Fasten off.

CROCHETING APRON EDGES

With RS facing, waist strap to your right, and Yarn B, insert hook in 115th dc (joining point) of waist strap, *picot, sl st in next dc (ch-3) space. Rep from * 32 times, along one side of apron, from top to bottom. Cont and **picot, sk next dc, sl st in next dc. Rep from ** 27 times, then rep from * 32 times along other side of apron. Fasten off.

SUNFLOWER

Flower

With Yarn C, ch 5, join with sl st in 1st ch to form a ring.

Rnd 1: Ch 1, 8 sc in ring. Join with sl st in 1st sc.

Rnd 2: Ch 1, inserting hook in back lp only, 2 sc in same sc as joining and in each rem sc. Join with sl st in 1st sc —16 sc.

Rnd 3: Ch 1, inserting hook in back lp only, sc in same sc as joining, 2 sc in next sc, *sc in next sc, 2 sc in next sc. Rep from * 7 times. Join with sl st in 1st sc—24 sc.

Rnd 4: Ch 1, inserting hook in back lp only, sc in same sc as joining and in next sc, 2 sc in next sc, *sc in each of next 2 sc, 2 sc in next sc. Rep from * 7 times. Join with sl st in 1st sc—32 sc.

Rnd 5: Ch 1, inserting hook in back lp only, sc in same sc as joining and in each of next 2 sc, 2 sc in next sc, *sc in each of next 3 sc, 2 sc in next sc. Rep from * 7 times. Join with sl st in 1st sc—40 sc.

Rnd 6: Ch 1, inserting hook in back lp only, sc in same sc as joining and in each of next 3 sc, 2 sc in next sc, *sc in each of next 4 sc, 2 sc in next sc. Rep from * 7 times. Join with sl st in 1st sc—48 sc.

Rnd 7: Ch 1, inserting hook in back lp only, sc in same sc as joining and in each of next 4 sc, 2 sc in next sc, *sc in each of next 5 sc, 2 sc in next sc. Rep from * 7 times. Join with sl st in 1st sc—56 sc. Cut yarn.

Rnd 8: Join Yarn D, picot, sk joining st, *sl st in next sc, picot, sk next sc. Rep from * 27 times. Join with sl st in joining st of prev rnd. Fasten off.

Stem

Row 1: With Yarn B, ch 55 (stem); ch 12, working back, sl st in 1st ch from hook and in each of next 10 chs, sl st in prev ch of stem (1st leaf); ch 4 (stem); ch 20, working back, sl st in 1st ch from hook and in each of next 18 chs, sl st in prev ch of stem (2nd leaf); ch 6 (stem). Leave lp on hook. With RS of flower facing and joining st away from you, insert hook in 7th rnd joining st of flower, ch 1, sl st in 1st ch from hook and in each of next 64 chs along stem. Fasten off.

ATTACHING SUNFLOWER

With RS of apron and sunflower facing, and bottom of apron close to you, place flower about 3"/7.5cm from apron top, and 2"/5cm from one side of apron, and pin. Position stem and leaves as desired, and pin. With WS of apron facing, sew on in a few places with whip stitches that are not visible on RS.

PROTECTIVE PLASTIC COVER

Note: This cover is designed to protect the apron while you cook. Shaped like the apron but a bit larger, it has a large space at the top for inserting the apron, and a small space on either side for drawing out the apron straps.

TEMPLATE

Place tissue paper on work surface, and mark middle top on longer side. Measure 8½"/21.5cm on either side of middle top, and mark. Draw a line from mark on right side to bottom right corner. Draw a line from mark on left side to bottom left corner. Cut along lines to make a trapezoid shape.

Fold trapezoid in half lengthwise. With folded side to the right, measure 3"/7.5cm to the left along top from top folded corner, and mark. Measure ⅛"/0.3mm below top along folded side, then draw a 3"/7.5cm line, parallel to the top, and mark. Draw a line upwards to connect the two marks. Draw an arc on unfolded bottom corner. With paper still folded, cut along arc to make even rounded corners on both sides of bottom. Cut out rectangle at top of template, to remove a ⅛"/0.3mm x 6"/15.2cm rectangle from top.

Unfold template.

PLASTIC COVER

Fold transparent plastic in half widthwise. Place template on plastic, with template top corresponding to folded side of plastic. Trace, then cut plastic.

With plastic folded, starting 2"/5cm down from top of cover (folded part), and using leather hole punch, punch holes ¼"/0.6cm from edge of cover, and about ¼"/0.6cm apart, along one side of cover, bottom, and other side, until 2"/5cm from the top.

CROCHETING COVER EDGES

With front of cover facing, top to your right, and Yarn B, insert hook in rightmost holes of cover front and back, *picot, sl st in next pair holes of cover front and back. Rep from * along cover one side, bottom, and other side. Fasten off.

Insert apron into space at top of cover, and draw apron straps out of spaces at sides of cover.

this project was crocheted with

(A) 2 balls of Red Heart Eco-Cotton Blend, 75% recycled cotton/25% acrylic, medium weight, approx 3oz/85g = 145yd/132m per ball, color 1373

(B) 1 ball of Lion Cotton-Ease® (new) Yarn, 50% cotton/50% acrylic, medium worsted weight, approx 3.5oz/100g = 207yd/188m per ball, color 830-132

(C) 1 ball of Red Heart Eco-Cotton Blend, 75% recycled cotton/25% acrylic, medium weight, approx 3oz/85g = 145yd/132m per ball, 1360

(D) 1 ball of Lion Cotton-Ease® (new) Yarn, 50% cotton/50% acrylic, medium worsted weight, approx 3.5oz/100g = 207yd/188m per ball, color 830-186

earthy oven mitt

This oven mitt will protect your hand when you take hot items out of the oven. With its pretty eyelet, it can be hung on the wall when not in use, so it's always accessible.

EXPERIENCE LEVEL

◼◼◼▭ Intermediate

FINISHED MEASUREMENTS

- 8½"/21.5cm x 5"/12.5cm

MATERIALS AND TOOLS

- Yarn A  : 145yd/132m of Medium weight yarn, recycled cotton/acrylic, in dark brown
- Yarn B : 145yd/132m of Medium weight yarn, recycled cotton/acrylic, in light beige
- Yarn C : 207yd/188m of Medium Worsted weight yarn, cotton/acrylic, in dark olive green
- Size E/4 (3.5mm) crochet hook OR SIZE TO OBTAIN GAUGE
- Scissors

GAUGE

- With Yarn A, 12 sts and 10 rows = 2"/5cm in sc

SPECIAL STITCHES

- Picot: Ch 3, sl st in 1st ch of ch-3 (page 10)
- Overlay chain stitch (page 9)

instructions

PALM AND BACK OF HAND

Palm

With Yarn A, ch 31.

Row 1: Sc into 2nd ch from hook and in each of next 28 chs, 5 sc in last ch. Don't turn. Work along bottom side of foundation chs, sc in unused lps of next 29 chs—63 sc.

Row 2: Ch 1, inserting hook in front lp only, sc in 1st sc from hook and in each of next 28 sc, 2 sc in each of next 5 sc, sc in each of next 29 sc—68 sc.

Row 3: Ch 1, inserting hook in front lp only, sc in 1st sc from hook and in each of next 30 sc, 2 sc in each of next 6 sc, sc in each of next 31 sc—74 sc.

Row 4: Ch 1, inserting hook in front lp only, sc in 1st sc from hook and in each of next 33 sc, 2 sc in each of next 6 sc, sc in each of next 34 sc—80 sc.

Row 5: Ch 1, inserting hook in front lp only, sc in 1st sc from hook and in each of next 37 sc, 2 sc in each of next 4 sc, sc in each of next 38 sc—84 sc.

Row 6: Ch 1, inserting hook in front lp only, sc in 1st sc from hook and in each of next rem sc—84 sc.

Row 7: Ch 1, inserting hook in front lp only, sc in 1st sc from hook and in each of next 39 sc, 2 sc in each of next 4 sc, sc in each of next 40 sc—88 sc.

Row 8: Rep row 6.

Row 9: Ch 1, inserting hook in front lp only, sc in 1st sc from hook and in each of next 40 sc, 2 sc in each of next 6 sc, sc in each of next 41 sc—94 sc.

Row 10: Rep row 6.

Row 11: Ch 1, inserting hook in front lp only, sc in 1st sc from hook and in each of next 43 sc, 2 sc in each of next 6 sc, sc in each of next 44 sc—100 sc.

Row 12: Rep row 6. Fasten off.

Back of hand

With Yarn B, ch 31.

Rows 1–10: With Yarn B, rep rows 1–10 of palm.

Rows 11–12: Join Yarn A and rep rows 11–12 of palm.

CROCHETED PIPING

With RS of back of hand facing and Yarn C, insert hook in 2nd sc at 9th row of back of hand. Work overlay chs in each of next 92 sc (until 2nd to last sc) along 9th row of back of hand. Cont and work overlay chs in each of next 18 sc along mitt bottom. Fasten off.

THUMB (Make 2)

With Yarn A, ch 13.

Row 1: Sc into 2nd ch from hook and in each of next 10 chs, 5 sc in last ch. Don't turn. Work along bottom side of foundation chs, sc in unused lps of next 10 chs. Don't sc in last ch—26 sc.

Row 2: Ch 1, inserting hook in front lp only, sc in 1st sc from hook and in each of next 9 sc, 2 sc in each of next 5 sc, sc in each of next 10 sc, 2 sc in last sc—32 sc.

Row 3: Ch 1, inserting hook in front lp only, sc in 1st sc from hook and in each of next 13 sc, 2 sc in each of next 6 sc, sc in each of next 11 sc. Don't sc in last sc—37 sc.

Row 4: Ch 1, inserting hook in front lp only, sc in 1st sc from hook and in each of next 35 sc, 2 sc in last sc—38 sc. Fasten off.

ATTACHING PARTS

Attaching thumb for right (left) hander

With WS of palm facing, mitt bottom to your left (right), and thumb angled to the right (left), place thumb bottom on last row of far side of palm, with right edge of thumb at 18th (10th) sc from bottom of palm. With Yarn A, insert hook in rightmost st at thumb bottom and in 18th (10th) sc from bottom of palm. Work overlay chs in each of next

8 sts along thumb bottom and its corresponding sc along last row of palm. Fasten off.

With WS of back of hand facing, mitt bottom to your right (left), thumb angled to the left (right), place thumb bottom on last row of far side of back of hand, with right edge of thumb at 10th (18th) sc from bottom of back of hand. With Yarn A, insert hook in rightmost st at thumb bottom and in 10th (18th) sc from bottom of back of hand. Work overlay chs in each of next 8 sts along thumb bottom and its corresponding sc along last row of back of hand. Fasten off.

Attaching palm and back of hand for right (left) hander

Place palm and back of hand with WS tog. With RS of back of hand facing, mitt bottom to your right (left), and Yarn C, insert hook in rightmost sc at last row of back of hand and its corresponding sc at last row of palm. Work overlay chs in each of next pairs along last row of back of hand, until thumb. Then work overlay chs in each of next pairs along last row of thumb. Cont and work overlay chs in each of next rem pairs along last row of back of hand. Fasten off.

CROCHETING MITT BOTTOM

Rnd 1: With RS of palm facing, mitt bottom away from you, and Yarn A, insert hook in rightmost edge st at palm bottom, ch 1, sc in same st and in each of next edge st around mitt bottom. Join with sl st in 1st sc.

Rnd 2: Ch 1, sc in same sc as joining and in each rem sc. Join with sl st in 1st sc.

Fasten off.

FLOWERY EYELET FOR RIGHT (LEFT) HANDER

Center

With RS of back of hand facing, mitt bottom to your right (left), and Yarn A, insert hook through top st at 1st rnd of crocheted mitt bottom, ch 12. End with sl st in same top st. Fasten off.

Petals

With Yarn C, insert hook in 1st ch of eyelet, picot; *sk next ch, sl st in next ch, picot. Rep from * 5 times. Join with sl st in 1st ch of eyelet. Fasten off.

this project was crocheted with

(A) 1 ball of Red Heart Eco-Cotton Blend, 75% recycled cotton/25% acrylic, medium weight, approx 3oz/85g = 145yd/132m per ball, color 1360

(B) 1 ball of Red Heart Eco-Cotton Blend, 75% recycled cotton/25% acrylic, medium weight, approx 3oz/85g = 145yd/132m per ball, color 1340

(C) 1 ball of Lion Cotton-Ease® (new) Yarn, 50% cotton/50% acrylic, medium worsted weight, approx 3.5oz/100g = 207yd/188m per ball, color 830-132

large gourd container

With their shapely form and diverse colors, gourds are often carved, hollowed out, and used as ornaments and containers. In this container, the color and shape resembles a dry gourd. For a smaller version of this design, see page 102.

EXPERIENCE LEVEL

■■■□ Intermediate

FINISHED MEASUREMENTS

- 6¼"/16cm diameter at bottom x 9"/23cm tall (with cover)

MATERIALS AND TOOLS

- Yarn A  : 103yd/94m of Worsted weight yarn, organic cotton, in deep brown

- Yarn B (4): 103yd/94m of Worsted weight yarn, organic cotton, in dark green

- Yarn C (2): 21.9yd/20m of Thin, 3-strand hemp yarn, in natural beige

- Rope: 55yd/50m of Multi-ply jute twine, approx ³/₁₆"/5mm diameter, in natural beige

- Size E/4 (3.5mm) crochet hook OR SIZE TO OBTAIN GAUGE

- Scissors

GAUGE

- With Yarn A, 8 sts and 7 rows = 2"/5cm in sc over rope

SPECIAL STITCHES

- Reverse single crochet stitch (page 10)

TECHNIQUES

- Foundation row over rope (page 14)

- Foundation round over rope (page 15)

- Single crochet over rope (page 16)

- Chain above rope, single crochet over rope (page 16)

- Long single crochet over rope (page 17)

instructions

ROUND BASE

Foundation row: With free end of rope to your right and Yarn A, ch 1 over rope (leaving 1"/2.5cm tail of rope), 8 sc along and over rope.

Rnd 1: Curve foundation row into a ring, and carry rope and yarn above foundation row to connect ring by making 2 sc over rope into 1st sc of foundation row. Curving rope around foundation row, 2 sc over rope in each of next 7 sc—16 sc.

Note: Curve rope around each of next rounds, following instructions below, to make a round shape.

Rnd 2: *Sc over rope in next sc, 2 sc over rope in next sc. Rep from * 8 times—24 sc.

Rnd 3: *Sc over rope in each of next 2 sc, 2 sc over rope in next sc. Rep from * 8 times—32 sc.

Rnd 4: *Sc over rope in each of next 3 sc, 2 sc over rope in next sc. Rep from * 8 times—40 sc.

Rnd 5: *Sc over rope in each of next 4 sc, 2 sc over rope in next sc. Rep from * 8 times—48 sc.

Rnd 6: *Sc over rope in each of next 5 sc, 2 sc over rope in next sc. Rep from * 8 times—56 sc.

Rnd 7: *Sc over rope in each of next 6 sc, 2 sc over rope in next sc. Rep from * 8 times—64 sc.

Rnd 8: (Sc over rope, ch 1 above rope) all in each of next 64 sc—64 sc and 64 ch-1 spaces.

Rnd 9: (Sc over rope, ch 1 above rope) all in each of next 64 ch-1 spaces—64 sc and 64 ch-1 spaces. Cut yarn.

BODY

Note: Curve rope above each of next rounds, following instructions below.

Rnds 10–15: Join Yarn A, and rep rnd 9.

Note: Curve rope above each of next rounds, making each next round narrower than previous, and following instructions below.

Rnd 16: *Sc over rope in each of next 2 ch-1 spaces, ch 1 above rope. Rep from * 32 times—64 sc and 32 ch-1 spaces.

Rnd 17: *Sc over rope in next sc, sk next sc, sc over rope in next ch-1 space. Rep from * 32 times—64 sc.

Rnd 18: Sc over rope in each of next 64 sc.

Rnd 19: *Sc over rope in each of next 7 sc, sk next sc. Rep from * 8 times—56 sc.

Rnd 20: Sc over rope in each of next 56 sc.

Rnd 21: *Sc over rope in each of next 6 sc, sk next sc. Rep from * 8 times—48 sc.

Rnd 22: Sc over rope in each of next 48 sc. Join with sl st in 1st sc. Cut yarn and rope. Fasten rope in place.

Rnd 23: Join Yarn B, ch 1, sc in same st as joining and in each of next rem sc—48 sc.

Rnd 24: Working left to right, ch 1, reverse sc in same st as joining and in each of next rem sc—48 reverse sc. Join with sl st in 1st reverse sc. Fasten off.

COVER

Foundation row: With free end of rope to your right and Yarn A, ch 1 over rope (leaving 10"/25.5cm tail of rope for later use), 8 sc along and over rope.

Rnd 1: Rep rnd 1 of round base.

Note: Curve rope above each of next rounds, making each next round wider than previous, and following instructions below.

Rnd 2: Sc over rope in each of next 16 sc.

Rnd 3: Rep rnd 2 of round base.

Rnd 4: Sc over rope in each of next 24 sc.

Rnd 5: Rep rnd 3 of round base—32 sc.

Rnd 6: Sc over rope in each of next 32 sc.

Rnd 7: Join Yarn A, *sc over rope in next sc, lsc over rope in next sc 1 rnd below. Rep from * 16 times—16 sc and 16 lsc.

Rnd 8: *Sc over rope in each of next 32 sts—32 sc.

Rnd 9: Rep rnd 4 of round base—40 sc.

Rnds 10–11: Sc over rope in each of next 40 sc.

Rnd 12: Rep rnd 5 of round base—48 sc.

Rnds 13–14: Sc over rope in each of next 48 sc.

Rnd 15: Rep rnd 6 of round base—56 sc.

Rnd 16: Rep rnd 7 of round base. Join with sl st in 1st sc. Cut rope and fasten in place.

Rnd 17: Working left to right, ch 1, reverse sc in same st as joining and in each of next rem sc—64 reverse sc. Join with sl st in 1st reverse sc. Fasten off.

STEM

Fold rope tail at top of cover, so that free end of tail extends 1"/2.5cm beyond base of stem. With one hand, hold folded rope and 3"/7.5cm of free end of Yarn C tog (ball of Yarn C is in other hand). Starting ½"/1.3cm down from top, wrap Yarn C tightly over folded rope and hemp yarn tail, then cont wrapping folded rope all the way to base of stem. With Yarn C, tie an overhand knot. Cut yarn, leaving a 1"/2.5cm tail. Hide rope and yarn tail inside cover and fasten in place.

ATTACHING COVER TO THE BODY

Place cover on top of body, with its 17th rnd joining st matching same st at 23rd rnd of body. With Yarn A, insert hook in 6th st to right of joining st at 17th rnd of cover,

and corresponding st at 23rd rnd of body. Work 12 overlay chs, inserting hook in each of next 12 pairs of sts along 17th rnd of cover and corresponding 23rd rnd of body. Fasten off.

this project was crocheted with

(A) 2 balls of Lion Nature's Choice Organic Cotton Yarn, 100% organic cotton, worsted weight, approx 3oz/85g = 103yd/94m per ball, color 480-125

(B) 1 ball of Lion Nature's Choice Organic Cotton Yarn, 100% organic cotton, worsted weight, approx 3oz/85g = 103yd/94m per ball, color 480-123

(C) 1 spool of HempBasics, 100% hemp 3-strand yarn, approx 17.6oz/500g = 1800yd/ 1642m per spool

(Rope) 3-ply jute twine, 100% jute, approx ³⁄₁₆"/5mm diameter, in natural beige

small gourd container

Gourds are one of nature's most wondrous vegetables, coming in an endless variety of shapes and sizes. This gourd-shaped container is perfect for holding diverse items stylishly and discretely. For a larger version, see page 99.

EXPERIENCE LEVEL

■■■□ Intermediate

FINISHED MEASUREMENTS

- 4"/10cm diameter at bottom x 5"/12.5cm tall (with cover)

MATERIALS AND TOOLS

- Yarn A  : 103yd/94m of Worsted weight yarn, organic cotton, in deep brown
- Yarn B **MEDIUM 4** : 103yd/94m of Worsted weight yarn, organic cotton, in light green
- Yarn C **FINE 2** : 21.9yd/20m of Thin, 3-strand hemp yarn, in natural beige
- Rope: 44yd/40m of Multi-ply jute twine, approx 3/16"/5mm diameter, in natural beige
- Size E/4 (3.5mm) crochet hook OR SIZE TO OBTAIN GAUGE
- Scissors

GAUGE

- With Yarn A, 8 sts and 7 rows = 2"/5cm in sc over rope

SPECIAL STITCHES

- Reverse single crochet stitch (page 10)

TECHNIQUES

- Foundation row over rope (page 14)
- Foundation round over rope (page 15)
- Single crochet over rope (page 16)
- Chain above rope, single crochet over rope (page 16)
- Long single crochet over rope (page 17)

instructions

ROUND BASE

Foundation row: With Yarn B, rep foundation row of Large Gourd Container round base.

Rnds 1–4: Rep rnds 1–4 of Large Gourd Container round base.

Rnd 5: (Sc over rope, ch 1 above rope) all in each of next 40 sc—40 sc and 40 ch-1 spaces. Cut yarn.

BODY

Rnds 6–10: Join Yarn A, (sc over rope, ch 1 above rope) all in each of next 40 ch-1 spaces—40 sc and 40 ch-1 spaces.

Rnd 11: *Sc over rope in each of next 2 ch-1 spaces, ch 1 above rope. Rep from * 20 times—40 sc and 20 ch-1 spaces.

Rnd 12: *Sc over rope in next sc, sk next sc, sc over rope in next ch-1 space. Rep from * 20 times—40 sc.

Rnds 13–14: Sc over rope in each of next 40 sc. Join with sl st in 1st sc. Cut yarn and rope. Fasten rope in place.

Rnd 15: Join Yarn B, ch 1, sc in same st as joining and in each of next rem sc—40 sc.

Rnd 16: Working left to right, ch 1, reverse sc in same st as joining and in each of next rem sc—40 reverse sc. Join with sl st in 1st reverse sc. Fasten off.

COVER

Foundation row: With free end of rope to your right and Yarn A, ch 1 over rope (leaving 10"/25.5cm tail of rope for later use), 8 sc along and over rope.

Rnd 1: Rep rnd 1 of round base.

Note: Curve rope above each of next rounds, making each next round wider than previous, and following instructions below:

Rnds 2–3: Sc over rope in each of next 16 sc.

Rnd 4: *Sc over rope in next sc, 2 sc over rope in next sc. Rep from * 8 times—24 sc.

Rnds 5–6: Sc over rope in each of next 24 sc.

Rnd 7: Join Yarn A, *sc over rope in next sc, lsc over rope in next sc 1 rnd below. Rep from * 12 times—12 sc and 12 lsc.

Rnd 8: *Sc over rope in each of next 2 sts, 2 sc over rope in next st. Rep from * 8 times—32 sc.

Rnd 9: Sc over rope in each of next 32 sc.

Rnd 10: *Sc over rope in each of next 3 sc, 2 sc over rope in next sc. Rep from * 8 times—40 sc.

Rnd 11: Sc over rope in each of next 40 sc.

Rnd 12: *Sc over rope in each of next 4 sc, 2 sc over rope in next sc. Rep from * 8 times—48 sc.

Rnd 13: Sc over rope in each of next 48 sc. Join with sl st in 1st sc. Cut rope and fasten in place.

Rnd 14: Working left to right, ch 1, reverse sc in same st as joining and in each of next rem sc—48 reverse sc. Join with sl st in 1st reverse sc. Fasten off.

STEM

Follow same instruction as for Large Gourd Container (page 101).

ATTACHING COVER TO THE BODY

Place cover on top of body, with 13th rnd joining st matching same st at 15th rnd of body. With Yarn A, insert hook in 5th st to right of joining st at 13th rnd of cover and corresponding st at 15th rnd of body. Work 10 overlay chs, inserting hook in each of next 10 pairs of sts along 13th rnd of cover and corresponding 15th rnd of body. Fasten off.

this project was crocheted with

(A) 1 ball of Lion Nature's Choice Organic Cotton Yarn, 100% organic cotton, worsted weight, approx 3oz/85g = 103yd/94m per ball, color 480-125

(B) 1 ball of Lion Nature's Choice Organic Cotton Yarn, 100% organic cotton, worsted weight, approx 3oz/85g = 103yd/94m per ball, color 480-169

(C) 1 spool of HempBasics, 100% hemp 3-strand yarn, approx 17.6oz/500g = 1800yd/ 1642m per spool

(Rope) 3-ply jute twine, 100% jute, approx ³⁄₁₆"/5mm diameter, in natural beige

flexible flower vase

With earth tones like the soil in which flowers grow, this malleable vase is ideal for holding fresh flowers and leaves. Simply place a small jar or bottle inside, for holding fresh water.

EXPERIENCE LEVEL

■■■ ▭ Intermediate

FINISHED MEASUREMENTS

- 7"/18cm diameter at bottom x 11"/28cm tall

MATERIALS AND TOOLS

- Yarn A  : 103yd/94m of Worsted weight yarn, organic cotton, in light brown

- Yarn B  : 103yd/94m of Worsted weight yarn, organic cotton, in light beige

- Rope: 44yd/40m of Multi-ply jute twine, approx ³⁄₁₆"/5mm diameter, in natural beige

- Size E/4 (3.5mm) crochet hook OR SIZE TO OBTAIN GAUGE

- Scissors

GAUGE

- With Yarn A, 8 sts and 7 rows = 2"/5cm in sc over rope

SPECIAL STITCHES

- Reverse single crochet stitch (page 10)

TECHNIQUES

- Attaching rope to foundation chains (page 15)

- Single crochet over rope (page 16)

instructions

OVAL BASE

Foundation row: With Yarn A, ch 15.

With free end of rope to your right, attach rope to foundation row as follows:

Rnd 1: 5 Sc over rope in 2nd ch from hook, sc over rope in each of next 13 chs, 5 sc over rope in last ch. Don't turn.

Curving rope around, work along bottom side of foundation chs, sc over rope in unused lps of next 13 chs—36 sc.

Note: Curve rope around each of next rounds, making an oval shape, and following instructions below.

Rnd 2: *2 sc over rope in each of next 5 sc, sc over rope in each of next 13 sc. Rep from * twice—46 sc.

Rnd 3: Sc over rope in each of next 3 sc, 2 sc over rope in each of next 4 sc, sc over rope in each of next 19 sc, 2 sc over rope in each of next 4 sc, sc over rope in each of next 16 sc—54 sc.

Rnd 4: Join Yarn B, sc over rope in each of next 5 sc, 2 sc over rope in each of next 4 sc, sc over rope in each of next 23 sc, 2 sc over rope in each of next 4 sc, sc over rope in each of next 18 sc—62 sc.

Rnd 5: With Yarn A, sc over rope in each of next 8 sc, 2 sc over rope in each of next 2 sc, sc over rope in each of next 29 sc, 2 sc over rope in each of next 2 sc, sc over rope in each of next 21 sc—66 sc.

Rnd 6: With Yarn B, sc over rope in each of next 9 sc, 2 sc over rope in each of next 2 sc, sc over rope in each of next 31 sc, 2 sc over rope in each of next 2 sc, sc over rope in each of next 22 sc—70 sc.

Rnd 7: With Yarn A, sc over rope in each of next 10 sc, 2 sc over rope in each of next 2 sc, sc over rope in each of next 33 sc, 2 sc over rope in each of next 2 sc, sc over rope in each of next 23 sc—74 sc.

Rnd 8: With Yarn B, sc over rope in each of next 11 sc, 2 sc over rope in each of next 2 sc, sc over rope in each of next 35 sc, 2 sc over rope in each of next 2 sc, sc over rope in each of next 24 sc—78 sc.

SHAPEABLE BODY

Note: Curve rope above each of next rounds, following instructions below.

Rnds 9–11: With Yarn A, sc over rope in each of next 78 sc.

Rnd 12: With Yarn B, *(sc over rope in each of next 3 sc, lsc over rope in each of next 3 sc 1 rnd below). Rep from * 13 times—39 sc and 39 lsc. Cut yarn.

Rnd 13: With Yarn A, *(lsc over rope in each of next 3 sc 1 rnd below, sc over rope in each of next 3 lsc). Rep from * 13 times—39 sc and 39 lsc.

Rnd 14: Sc over rope in each of next 78 sts.

Note: Curve rope above each of next rounds, making each next round narrower than previous, and following instructions below.

Rnd 15: *Sc over rope in each of next 26 sc, sk next sc, sc over rope in each of next 11 sc, sk next sc. Rep from * twice—74 sc.

Rnd 16: *Sc over rope in each of next 26 sc, sk next sc, sc over rope in each of next 9 sc, sk next sc. Rep from * twice—70 sc.

Rnd 17: Join Yarn B, *sc over rope in each of next 26 sc, sk next sc, sc over rope in each of next 7 sc, sk next sc. Rep from * twice—66 sc.

Rnd 18: With Yarn A, *sc over rope in each of next 26 sc, sk next sc, sc over rope in each of next 5 sc, sk next sc. Rep from * twice—62 sc.

Rnd 19: With Yarn B, *sc over rope in each of next 26 sc, sk next sc, sc over rope in each of next 3 sc, sk next sc. Rep from * twice—58 sc.

Rnd 20: With Yarn A, *sc over rope in each of next 26 sc, sk next sc, sc over rope in each of next 1 sc, sk next sc. Rep from * twice—54 sc.

Rnd 21: With Yarn B, sc over rope in each of next 10 sc, sk next sc, sc over rope in each of next 4 sc, sk next sc, sc over rope in each of next 21 sc, sk next sc, sc over rope in each of next 4 sc, sk next sc, sc over rope in each of next 11 sc—50 sc.

Rnd 22: With Yarn A, sc over rope in each of next 9 sc, sk next sc, sc over rope in each of next 4 sc, sk next sc, sc over rope in each of next 19 sc, sk next sc, sc over rope in each of next 4 sc, sk next sc, sc over rope in each of next 10 sc—46 sc.

Rnd 23: With Yarn B, sc over rope in each of next 8 sc, sk next sc, sc over rope in each of next 4 sc, sk next sc, sc over rope in each of next 17 sc, sk next sc, sc over rope in each of next 4 sc, sk next sc, sc over rope in each of next 9 sc—42 sc.

Rnd 24: With Yarn A, sc over rope in each of next 7 sc, sk next sc, sc over rope in each of next 4 sc, sk next sc, sc over rope in each of next 15 sc, sk next sc, sc over rope in each of next 4 sc, sk next sc, sc over rope in each of next 8 sc—38 sc.

Rnd 25: With Yarn B, sc over rope in each of next 6 sc, sk next sc, sc over rope in each of next 4 sc, sk next sc, sc over rope in each of next 13 sc, sk next sc, sc over rope in each of next 4 sc, sk next sc, sc over rope in each of next 7 sc—34 sc.

Rnd 26: With Yarn A, sc over rope in each of next 5 sc, sk next sc, sc over rope in each of next 4 sc, sk next sc, sc over rope in each of next 11 sc, sk next sc, sc over rope in each of next 4 sc, sk next sc, sc over rope in each of next 6 sc—30 sc.

Rnd 27: With Yarn B, sc over rope in each of next 4 sc, sk next sc, sc over rope in each of next 4 sc, sk next sc, sc over rope in each of next 9 sc, sk next sc, sc over rope in each of next 4 sc, sk next sc, sc over rope in each of next 5 sc—26 sc.

Note: Curve rope above each of next rounds, following instructions below.

Rnds 28–36: With Yarn A, sc over rope in each of next 26 sc.

Note: Curve rope above each of next rounds, making each next round wider than previous, and following instructions below.

Rnd 37: Sc over rope in each of next 3 sc, 2 sc over rope in next sc, sc over rope in each of next 4 sc, 2 sc over rope in next sc, sc over rope in each of next 7 sc, 2 sc over rope in next sc, sc over rope in each of next 4 sc, 2 sc over rope in next sc, sc over rope in each of next 4 sc—30 sc.

Rnd 38: Sc over rope in each of next 30 sc.

Rnd 39: Sc over rope in each of next 4 sc, 2 sc over rope in next sc, sc over rope in each of next 4 sc, 2 sc over rope in next sc, sc over rope in each of next 9 sc, 2 sc over rope in next sc, sc over rope in each of next 4 sc, 2 sc over rope in next sc, sc over rope in each of next 5 sc—34 sc.

Rnd 40: Sc over rope in each of next 34 sc. Join with sl st in 1st sc. Cut rope and fasten in place.

Rnd 41: Working left to right, ch 1, reverse sc in same st as joining and in each of next rem sc—34 reverse sc. Join with sl st in 1st reverse sc. Fasten off.

this project was crocheted with

(A) 2 balls of Lion Nature's Choice Organic Cotton Yarn, 100% organic cotton, worsted weight, approx 3oz/85g = 103yd/94m per ball, color 480-124

(B) 1 ball of Lion Nature's Choice Organic Cotton Yarn, 100% organic cotton, worsted weight, approx 3oz/85g = 103yd/94m per ball, color 480-099

(Rope) 3-ply jute twine, 100% jute, approx ³⁄₁₆"/5mm diameter, in natural beige

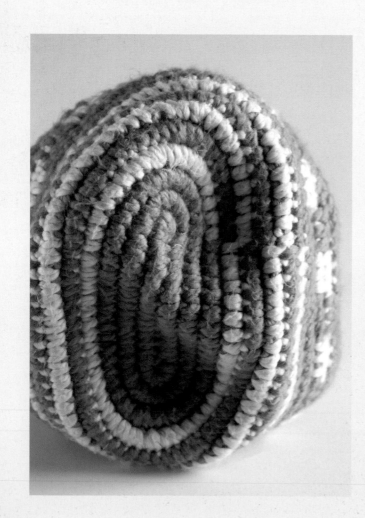

chamomile

Few things are as beautiful as a bouquet of wild flowers. This crocheted chamomile, along with the flower and leaf projects on the following pages, make a bouquet that is fresh and vibrant all year long. All of these projects feature flexible stems that can be bent, twirled, and wrapped.

EXPERIENCE LEVEL

■—■—□—□ Easy

FINISHED MEASUREMENTS

- Flower: Approx 4½"/11.5cm diameter
- Stem: 21"/53cm

MATERIALS AND TOOLS

- Yarn A **SUPER BULKY 6**: 103yd/94m of Bulky weight yarn, bamboo/acrylic/polyester, in cream
- Yarn B **SUPER BULKY 6**: 103yd/94m of Bulky weight yarn, bamboo/acrylic/polyester, in light yellow
- Yarn C **FINE 2**: 11yd/10m of Thin, 3-strand hemp yarn, in natural beige
- Rope: 40"/101.5cm of Multi-ply jute twine, approx ³⁄₁₆"/5mm diameter, in natural beige
- One piece of 18-gauge half-hard round steel wire, 22"/56cm long
- Size E/4 (3.5mm) crochet hook OR SIZE TO OBTAIN GAUGE
- Scissors
- Wire cutters

GAUGE

- With Yarn B, 8 sts and 7 rows = 2"/5cm in sc over rope

TECHNIQUES

- Foundation row over rope (page 14)
- Foundation round over rope (page 15)
- Single crochet over rope (page 16)
- Chain above rope, single crochet over rope (page 16)
- Crocheting petals in a round (page 18)
- Making a flexible stem with rootlets (page 19)

instructions

FLOWER CENTER

Foundation row: Starting 10"/25.5cm right from one end of rope, (with 30"/76cm end to your right), and Yarn B, ch 1 over rope, 11 sc along and over shorter rope end.

Rnd 1: Curving foundation row into a ring, and carrying short end of rope and yarn above longer end, connect ring by making 1 sc over shorter rope end into 1st sc of foundation row; ch 1 above shorter rope end. Curving shorter rope end around foundation row, (sc over shorter rope end, ch 1 above shorter rope end) all in each of next 9 sc; 2 sc over shorter rope end in last sc. Join with sl st in 1st sc—12 sc and 10 ch-1 spaces. Cut remainder of shorter rope end. Fasten off.

PETALS

With Yarn A, insert hook in joining st of rnd 1 of flower center, ch 1.

1st petal

Row 1: Sl st in 1st ch-1 space of rnd 1 of flower center, ch 8.

Row 2: Hdc into 2nd ch from hook and in next ch, sc in each of next 3 chs, sl st in next 2 chs and in 1st ch-1 space of rnd 1 of flower center. Don't cut yarn.

2nd (3rd) petal

Row 1: Sl st in 2nd (3rd) ch-1 space of rnd 1 of flower center, ch 9.

Row 2: Hdc into 2nd ch from hook and in each of next 2 chs, sc in each of next 3 chs, sl st in next 2 chs and in 2nd (3rd) ch-1 space of rnd 1 of flower center. Don't   cut yarn.

4th (5th, 6th) petal

Rep instructions for 1st petal, making 1st sl st of row 1 and last sl st of row 2 in 4th (5th, 6th) ch-1 space of rnd 1 of flower center.

7th (8th) petal

Rep instructions for 2nd (3rd) petal, making 1st sl st of row 1 and last sl st of row 2 in 7th (8th) ch-1 space of rnd 1 of flower center.

9th (10th) petal

Rep instructions for 1st petal, making 1st sl st of row 1 and last sl st of row 2, in 9th (10th) ch-1 space of rnd 1 of flower center.

11th petal

Row 1: Sk next sc of rnd 1 of flower center, sl st in last sc of rnd 1 of flower center, ch 7.

Row 2: Hdc into 2nd ch from hook and in next ch, sc in each of next 2 chs, sl st in next 2 chs and in last sc of rnd 1 of flower center.

End with sl st in 1st ch-1 space of rnd 1 of flower center. Fasten off.

STEM

With WS of flower facing, make an overhand knot flush against flower center in 30"/76cm rope end.

Insert 1"/2.5cm of wire in knot, from bottom of knot towards flower, and fold over thinner part of knot.

With flower to the right, holding rope, wire and 3"/7.5cm free end of Yarn C tog with one hand, use other hand to wrap Yarn C tightly, starting to the right of the knot, covering knot and folded wire, and cont along rope and wire all the way to end of wire.

With Yarn C, tie an overhand knot over rope. Cut Yarn C and rope, leaving a 5"/12.5cm tail on each.

ROOTLETS

Separate rope tail into three sections, and join Yarn C to one of the sections. Make an overhand knot in each section, flush against bottom of stem. Trim ends, leaving a 1"/2.5cm tail on each, and fray.

this project was crocheted with

(A) 1 ball of Bernat Bamboo Natural Blends, 86% bamboo/12% acrylic/2% polyester, bulky weight, approx 2.1oz/60g = 63yd/57m per ball, color 92008

(B) 1 ball of Bernat Bamboo Natural Blends, 86% bamboo/12% acrylic/2% polyester, bulky weight, approx 2.1oz/60g = 63yd/57m per ball, color 92515

(C) 1 spool of HempBasics, 100% hemp 3-strand yarn, approx 17.6oz/500g = 1800yd/ 1642m per spool

(Rope) 3-ply jute twine, 100% jute, approx 3/16"/5mm diameter, in natural beige

yellow thistle

Though natural thistles may be prickly when touched, this crocheted thistle actually has a lovely texture. It is perfect for combining in a vase with other crocheted flowers.

EXPERIENCE LEVEL

■■□□ Easy

FINISHED MEASUREMENTS

- Thistle: Approx 1½"/4cm diameter

- Stem: 21"/53cm

MATERIALS AND TOOLS

- Yarn A **MEDIUM 4**: 103yd/94m of Worsted weight yarn, organic cotton, in dark yellow

- Yarn B **FINE 2**: 11yd/10m of Thin, 3-strand hemp yarn, in natural beige

- Rope: 40"/101.5cm of Multi-ply jute twine, approx ³⁄₁₆"/5mm diameter, in natural beige

- One piece of 18-gauge half-hard round steel wire, 22"/56cm long

- Size E/4 (3.5mm) crochet hook OR SIZE TO OBTAIN GAUGE

- Scissors

- Wire cutters

GAUGE

- With Yarn B, 8 sts and 7 rows = 2"/5cm in sc over rope

TECHNIQUES

- Foundation row over rope (page 14)

- Foundation round over rope (page 15)

- Single crochet over rope (page 16)

- Chain above rope, single crochet over rope (page 16)

- Crocheting petals in a round (page 18)

- Making a flexible stem with rootlets (page 19)

instructions

Foundation row: Starting 10"/25.5cm right from one end of rope, (with 30"/76cm end to your right), and Yarn A, ch 1 over rope, 8 sc along and over shorter rope end.

Rnd 1: Curving foundation row into ring, and carrying short end of rope and yarn above longer end, connect the ring by making 1 sc over shorter rope end into 1st sc of foundation row; ch 1 above shorter rope end. Curving shorter rope end around foundation row, (sc over shorter rope end, ch 1 above shorter rope end) all in each of next 7 sc—8 sc and 8 ch-1 spaces.

Rnd 2: Curving shorter rope end around rnd 1, 2 sc over shorter rope end in 1st ch-1 space and in each of next 7 ch-1 spaces—16 sc. Join with sl st in 1st sc. Fasten off.

Trim shorter rope end, leaving a 1"/2.5cm tail.

STEM

With Yarn B, follow same instructions as for Chamomile (page 113).

ROOTLETS

With Yarn B, follow same instructions as for Chamomile (page 113).

this project was crocheted with

(A) 1 ball of Lion Nature's Choice Organic Cotton Yarn, 100% organic cotton, worsted weight, approx 3oz/85g = 103yd/94m per ball, color 480-158

(B) 1 spool of HempBasics, 100% hemp 3-strand yarn, approx 17.6oz/500g = 1800yd/ 1642m per spool

(Rope) 3-ply jute twine, 100% jute, approx ³⁄₁₆"/5mm diameter, in natural beige

leaf cluster

Few flower bouquets are complete without a bit of greenery. This leaf cluster is so pretty, it is lovely enough to make a bouquet, all on its own.

EXPERIENCE LEVEL

■■□□ Easy

FINISHED MEASUREMENTS

- Thistle: Approx 1½"/4cm diameter

- Stem: 21"/53cm

MATERIALS AND TOOLS

- Yarn A (**4** MEDIUM): 103yd/94m of Worsted weight yarn, organic cotton, in bright green

- Yarn B (**2** FINE): 11yd/10m of Thin, 3-strand hemp yarn, in natural beige

- Rope: 40"/101.5cm of Multi-ply jute twine, approx ³⁄₁₆"/5mm diameter, in natural beige

- One piece of 18-gauge half-hard round steel wire, 22"/56cm long

- Size E/4 (3.5mm) crochet hook OR SIZE TO OBTAIN GAUGE

- Scissors

- Wire cutters

GAUGE

- With Yarn B, 8 sts and 7 rows = 2"/5cm in sc over rope

TECHNIQUES

- Foundation row over rope (page 14)

- Foundation round over rope (page 15)

- Single crochet over rope (page 16)

- Chain above rope, single crochet over rope (page 16)

- Crocheting petals in a round (page 18)

- Making a flexible stem with rootlets (page 19)

instructions

Foundation row: Starting 10"/25.5cm right from one end of rope, (with 30"/76cm end to your right), and Yarn A, ch 1 over rope, 10 sc along and over shorter rope end.

Rnd 1(incomplete rnd): Curving foundation row into a ring, and carrying short end of rope and yarn above longer end, connect ring by making 2 sc over shorter rope end into 1st sc of foundation row. Curving shorter rope end around foundation row, 2 sc over shorter rope end, in each of next 6 sc—14 sc. Cut remainder of shorter rope end. Don't cut yarn.

LEAVES

1st leaf

Row 1: Sl st in next sc, ch 8.

Row 2: Sl st into 2nd ch from hook and in each of next 6 chs, sl st in same sc as at beg of row 1.

2nd leaf

Row 1: Sl st in next sc, ch 9.

Row 2: Sl st into 2nd ch from hook and in each of next 7 chs, sl st in same sc as at beg of row 1.

3rd (4th) leaf

Row 1: Sl st in next sc, ch 10.

Row 2: Sl st into 2nd ch from hook and in each of next 8 chs, sl st in same sc as at beg of row 1.

5th leaf

Rep instructions for 2nd leaf.

6th leaf

Rep instructions for 1st leaf.

Fasten off.

STEM

With Yarn B, follow same instructions as for Chamomile (page 113).

ROOTLETS

With Yarn B, follow same instructions as for Chamomile (page 113).

---

this project was crocheted with

(A) 1 ball of Lion Nature's Choice Organic Cotton Yarn, 100% organic cotton, worsted weight, approx 3oz/85g = 103yd/94m per ball, color 480-170

(B) 1 spool of HempBasics, 100% hemp 3-strand yarn, approx 17.6oz/500g = 1800yd/ 1642m per spool

(Rope) 3-ply jute twine, 100% jute, approx ³⁄₁₆"/5mm diameter, in natural beige

chrysanthemum

With their abundance of petals, chrysanthemums are one of my favorite flowers. Internationally, they are symbols of royalty, truth, and love.

EXPERIENCE LEVEL

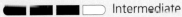 Intermediate

FINISHED MEASUREMENTS

- Flower: Approx 5"/25.5cm in diameter

- Stem: 21"/53cm

MATERIALS AND TOOLS

- Yarn A **4** (MEDIUM): 103yd/94m of Worsted weight yarn, organic cotton, in light brown

- Yarn B **4** (MEDIUM): 103yd/94m of Worsted weight yarn, organic cotton, in dusty blue

- Yarn C **2** (FINE): 11yd/10m of Thin, 3-strand hemp yarn, in natural beige

- Rope: 22"/56cm of Multi-ply jute twine, approx ³⁄₁₆"/5mm diameter, in natural beige

- One piece of 18 gauge half-hard round steel wire, 40"/101.5cm long

- Size E/4 (3.5mm) crochet hook OR SIZE TO OBTAIN GAUGE

- Scissors

- Wire cutters

GAUGE

- With Yarn B, 8 sts and 7 rows = 2"/5cm in sc over rope

TECHNIQUES

- Foundation row over rope (page 14)

- Foundation round over rope (page 15)

- Single crochet over rope (page 16)

- Crocheting petals in a round (page 18)

- Making a flexible stem with rootlets (page 19)

instructions

FLOWER CENTER

Foundation row: Starting 10"/25.5cm right from one end of rope, (with 30"/76cm end to your right), and Yarn A, ch 1 over rope, 10 sc along and over shorter rope end.

Rnd 1: Curving foundation row into a ring, and carrying short end of rope and yarn above longer end, connect ring by making 1 sc over shorter rope end, inserting hook in back lp only, into 1st sc of foundation row. Curving shorter rope end around foundation row and inserting hook in back lp only, 2 sc over shorter rope end; *sc over shorter rope end in next sc, 2 sc over shorter rope end in next sc. Rep from * 4 times—15 sc.

Rnd 2: Curving shorter rope end around 1st rnd and inserting hook in back lp only, *sc over shorter rope end in each of next 2 sc, 2 sc over shorter rope end in next sc. Rep from * 5 times. Join with sl st in 1st sc—20 sc. Cut remainder of shorter rope end. Fasten off.

STAMENS

With RS of flower center facing and Yarn A, insert hook, from top to bottom, in 10th (last) unused lp of flower center foundation row.

1st stamen

Row 1: Ch 6.

Row 2: Sl st into 2nd ch from hook and in each of next 4 chs, sl st in 10th unused lp of flower center foundation row.

2nd (3rd, 4th) stamen

Row 1: Sl st in 9th (8th, 7th) unused lp of flower center foundation row, ch 7.

Row 2: Sl st into 2nd ch from hook and in each of next 5 chs, sl st in 9th (8th, 7th) unused lp of flower center foundation row.

5th stamen

Row 1: Sl st in 6th unused lp of flower center foundation row, ch 8.

Row 2: Sl st into 2nd ch from hook and in each of next 6 chs, sl st in 6th unused lp of flower center foundation row.

6th stamen

Row 1: Sl st in 5th unused lp of flower center foundation row, ch 6.

Row 2: Sl st into 2nd ch from hook and in each of next 4 chs, sl st in 5th unused lp of flower center foundation row.

7th stamen

Rep instructions for 2nd stamen, making 1st sl st of row 1 and last sl st of row 2 in 4th unused lp of flower center foundation row.

8th stamen

Rep instructions for 6th stamen, making 1st sl st of row 1 and last sl st of row 2 in 3rd unused lp of flower center foundation row.

9th stamen

Rep instructions for 2nd stamen, making 1st sl st of row 1 and last sl st of row 2 in 2nd unused lp of flower center foundation row.

10th stamen

Rep instructions for 5th stamen, making 1st sl st of row 1 and last sl st of row 2 in 1st unused lp of flower center foundation row. End with sl st in 10th unused lp of flower center foundation row. Fasten off.

PETALS

With RS of flower center facing and Yarn B, insert hook, from top to bottom, in 15th (last) unused lp of rnd 1 of flower center.

1st petal

Row 1: Ch 7.

Row 2: Sl st into 2nd ch from hook and in each of next 5 chs, sl st in 15th unused lp of rnd 1 of flower center.

2nd (3rd, 4th) petal

Rep instructions for 5th stamen, making 1st sl st of row 1 and last sl st of row 2 in 14th (13th, 12th) unused lp of rnd 1 of flower center.

5th (6th) petal

Row 1: Sl st in 11th (10th) unused lp of rnd 1 of flower center, ch 9.

Row 2: Sl st into 2nd ch from hook and in each of next 7 chs, sl st in 11th (10th) unused lp of rnd 1 of flower center.

7th petal

Rep instructions for 2nd stamen, making 1st sl st of row 1 and last sl st of row 2 in 9th unused lp of rnd 1 of flower center.

8th (9th) petal

Rep instructions for 5th stamen, making 1st sl st of row 1 and last sl st of row 2 in 8th (7th) unused lp of rnd 1 of flower center.

10th petal

Rep instructions for 2nd stamen, making 1st sl st of row 1 and last sl st of row 2 in 6th unused lp of rnd 1 of flower center.

11th (12th) petal

Rep instructions for 5th stamen, making 1st sl st of row 1 and last sl st of row 2 in 5th (4th) unused lp of rnd 1 of flower center.

13th (14th and 15th) petal

Rep instructions for 5th stamen, making 1st sl st of row 1 and last sl st of row 2 in 3rd (2nd, 1st) unused lp of rnd 1 of flower center. End with sl st in 15th unused lp of rnd 1 of flower center. Fasten off.

STEM

With Yarn C, follow same instructions as for Chamomile (page 113).

ROOTLETS

With Yarn C, follow same instructions as for Chamomile (page 113).

---

this project was crocheted with

(A) 1 ball of Lion Nature's Choice Organic Cotton Yarn, 100% organic cotton, worsted weight, approx 3oz/85g = 103yd/94m per ball, color 480-124

(B) 1 ball of Lion Nature's Choice Organic Cotton Yarn, 100% organic cotton, worsted weight, approx 3oz/85g = 103yd/94m per ball, color 480-108

(C) 1 spool of HempBasics, 100% hemp 3-strand yarn, approx 17.6oz/500g = 1800yd/ 1642m per spool

(Rope) 3-ply jute twine, 100% jute, approx $\frac{3}{16}$"/5mm diameter, in natural beige

wind-blown chrysanthemum

This flower looks as though its colorful petals have been blown off by a strong autumn wind. Though only the stamens remain, the beauty of the flower isn't lost.

EXPERIENCE LEVEL

■■■□□ Easy

FINISHED MEASUREMENTS

- Flower: Approx 4"/10cm in diameter

- Stem: 21"/53cm

MATERIALS AND TOOLS

- Yarn A **4** MEDIUM: 103yd/94m of Worsted weight yarn, organic cotton, in light brown

- Yarn B **2** FINE: 11yd/10m of Thin, 3-strand hemp yarn, in natural beige

- Rope: 40"/101.5cm of Multi-ply jute twine, approx ³⁄₁₆"/5mm diameter, in natural beige

- One piece of 18-gauge half-hard round steel wire, 22"/56cm long

- Size E/4 (3.5mm) crochet hook OR SIZE TO OBTAIN GAUGE

- Scissors

- Wire cutters

GAUGE

- With Yarn B, 8 sts and 7 rows = 2"/5cm in sc over rope

TECHNIQUES

- Foundation row over rope (page 14)

- Foundation round over rope (page 15)

- Single crochet over rope (page 16)

- Crocheting petals in a round (page 18)

- Making a flexible stem with rootlets (page 19)

instructions

FLOWER CENTER

Foundation row and Rnd 1: Follow same instructions as for Chrysanthemum (page 120). Join with sl st in 1st sc—15 sc. Cut remainder of shorter rope end. Fasten off.

STAMENS

Follow same instructions as for Chrysanthemum (pages 120-121).

STEM

With Yarn B, follow same instructions as for Chamomile (page 113).

ROOTLETS

With Yarn B, follow same instructions as for Chamomile (page 113).

this project was crocheted with

(A) 1 ball of Lion Nature's Choice Organic Cotton Yarn, 100% organic cotton, worsted weight, approx 3oz/85g = 103yd/94m per ball, color 480-124

(B) 1 spool of HempBasics, 100% hemp 3-strand yarn, approx 17.6oz/500g = 1800yd/ 1642m per spool

(Rope) 3-ply jute twine, 100% jute, approx ³/₁₆"/5mm diameter, in natural beige

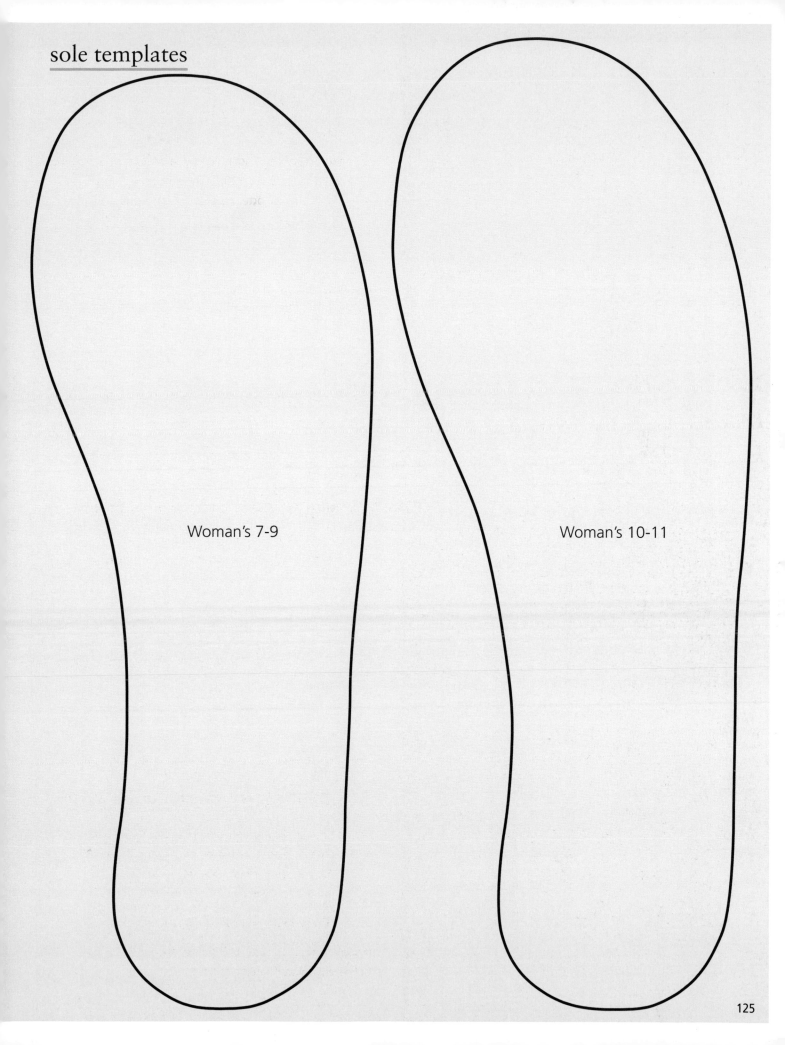

Woman's 7-9

Woman's 10-11

fields of farms diagram

Rotate book 90° to orient diagram correctly

row

181
180   170   160   150   140   130   120   110   100   90   80   70

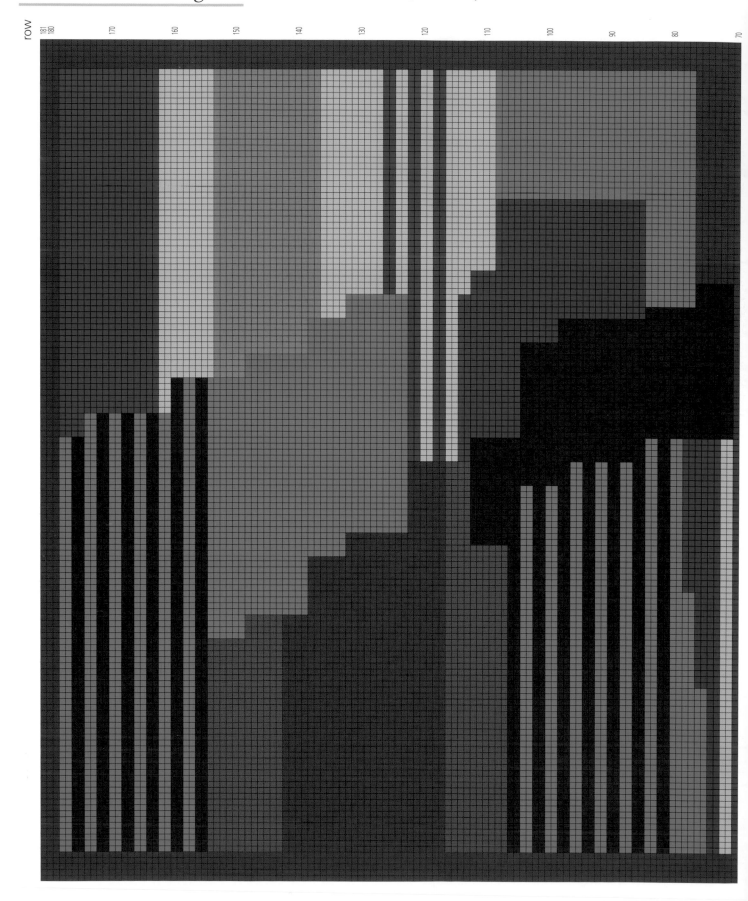

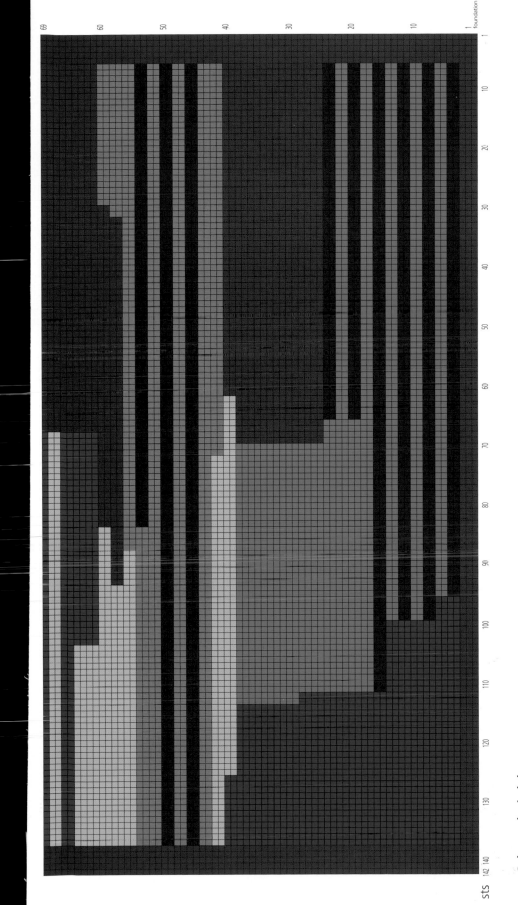

Color and stitch key

- ■ sc over rope with yarn A
- ■ sc over rope with yarn B
- ■ sc over rope with yarn C
- ■ sc over rope with yarn D
- ■ sc over rope with yarn E
- ■ sc over rope with yarn F
- ■ sc over rope with yarn G
- ■ sc over rope with yarn H

index